The Library Security and Safety Guide to Prevention, Planning, and Response

MIRIAM B. KAHN

American Library Association
Chicago 2008

Miriam B. Kahn has been working in the field of preservation since 1989 and founded MBK Consulting in 1991. She helps libraries, archives, other cultural institutions, and corporations plan for, recover from, and prevent disasters that interrupt services to the public. She writes about preservation and disaster response and teaches regularly for library consortia throughout the Midwest and at the School of Library and Information Science at Kent State University. Kahn is the author of *Disaster Response and Planning for Libraries* (2nd ed., 2003), *Protecting Your Library's Electronic Resources* (2004), and *First Steps for Handling and Drying Water Damaged Materials* (1994). She has served as preservation officer, State Library of Ohio; coordinator of online services, University of South Dakota; and reference librarian, New York Public Library. Kahn holds an MLS from Queens College and an MA in history from Hunter College.

The paper used in this publication meets the minimum requirements of American National Standard for Information Sciences—Permanence of Paper for Printed Library Materials, ANSI Z39.48-1992. ∞

Library of Congress Cataloging-in-Publication Data
Kahn, Miriam (Miriam B.)
The library security and safety guide to prevention, planning, and response / Miriam B. Kahn.
p. cm.
Includes bibliographical references and index.
ISBN 978-0-8389-0949-2 (alk. paper)
1. Libraries—Security measures. 2. Libraries—Safety measures. 3. Book thefts—Prevention. I. Title.
Z679.6K34 2008
025.8'2—dc22
2007050763

ISBN-13: 978-0-8389-0949-2
ISBN-10: 0-8389-0949-3

Printed in the United States of America
12 11 10 09 08 5 4 3 2 1

Contents

Acknowledgments

This book would not have been written or completed without the encouragement and assistance of my colleagues and friends. I would like to thank the following colleagues: Tanya Zanish-Belcher, head of Special Collections at Iowa State University Library, for suggestions for the numerous forms found in appendix B and for information she provided about managing the security of a special collections department; Karen Benedict, for providing information about security for archives and records centers; and Cynthia Read Miller, archivist at the Henry Ford Museum, for encouraging me to tackle this topic. My thanks to Thomas Simiele for the "Public Library Exhibitor Release Form" in appendix B. My extra thanks to Julie Callahan at the Columbus Metropolitan Library, who kept me informed about public libraries; to Nancy Birk and Cara Gilgenbach, my friends and colleagues at Kent State University Libraries, for talking about security issues in their Special Collections/Archives Department; and to Margaret Mauer, who just listened. Thanks to Richard Rubin, director of the School of Library and Information Science at Kent State University, for reigniting my interest in disasters and security and for giving me a place to teach about the topic. As always, I would like to thank my colleague Clark Searle for his insight into insurance issues for cultural institutions. I am ever grateful to my business partner Wayne Luff, who helped me carve time out of the business to write yet another book. Most of all, I would like to thank my former editor Marlene Chamberlain for asking me to write this book, and my current editor, Jenni Fry, who showed great faith in me.

Introduction

Every week there are articles in newspapers and professional journals and on the radio highlighting thefts and vandalism in libraries, archives, historical societies, and museums. Why are our cultural institutions targets for these crimes? And more important, how should we protect our buildings, materials, resources, users, and staff? The primary mission of our cultural institutions is to make the world's treasures in art, literature, science, and more available to anyone who wishes to see and use them. There will always be people, however, who test the mettle of librarians, archivists, and curators to protect these materials and who ultimately force restrictions on what was once freely accessible. In the course of our working day and our routines, how can we reduce the risk of damage, loss, and theft to our collections and therefore reduce the need for restriction? Are there also ways we can decrease injury and risk to our staff and patrons while they are in our buildings and on our grounds?

The very nature and concept of cultural institutions make their collections vulnerable to theft and their staff open to harm. Libraries and archives open their doors to all segments of society, providing information, entertainment, and education. These buildings are study areas for students of all ages; research resources and centers for businesspeople, teachers, and students; safe havens for the homeless and dispossessed; and much more. Historical societies and the special collections departments of libraries and archives contain artifacts, manuscripts, and unique items that historians and researchers of all types and in all disciplines examine. Museums house all of the above as well as priceless paintings, sculpture, and so much more.

The policies of open access common to many cultural institutions throughout the world make collections vulnerable to misuse and theft. Staff members bring objects out to users, trusting that these items will be returned in the same condition. At the same time, most cultural institutions, especially the smallest, have few safety measures in place, and therefore little or no ability to protect those who use the collections and those who work there.

In today's post-9/11 environment, we must plan for both the safety of our staff and patrons and the security of our collections. It is essential that we evaluate the potential for risk and the chance that someone will breach our security and safety systems. How much risk is there to the cultural institution you work in? To the staff? The collections? The digital resources? Even your patrons? Which parts of your collections and buildings are more vulnerable than others? How will you determine this and thus prevent the loss of irreplaceable resources?

This publication is designed to teach you how to survey your facilities and to protect the contents of your buildings from theft and damage. It also seeks to teach you how to protect your users and staff members from injury and inappropriate behavior by others. The three parts of this book cover security of buildings and grounds; security of general collections, equipment, and technology, including insurance considerations; and safety for staff and patrons.

Designed for all sizes and types of cultural institutions, this book takes a broad view of the problems and issues that affect most institutions. There will be issues and suggestions that are not relevant to your library, archive, historical society, or museum because of its physical size, its financial means, or some other factor. Nevertheless, the ideas behind the suggestions can inform your local actions and policies.

The checklists in appendix A are designed to help you create and perform building and security surveys, and to help you make decisions about security and safety measures. Appendix B includes sample forms you can adapt for your own use. Appendix C lists organizations that can help you in your efforts.

Because there have been many changes in the concepts and concerns of institutional security and safety since September 11, 2001, most of the books, articles, and websites in the bibliography are drawn from publications written after that date. Publications written prior to 2001 are included if they contain generic information or background material, or if they are still relevant in today's security-conscious environment.

A WORD ON MANAGING RISK IN CULTURAL INSTITUTIONS

Risk management is the evaluation and mitigation of, and response planning for, possible threats or risks. Each location and each department within your institution has a different level of threat or risk. Therefore, when thinking about the security of your collections and the safety of your users and staff, you must consider how each department can prevent risk and respond to its attendant problems, then integrate the needs of each department into the whole picture. You need to consider how your institution will react when faced with risk or loss.

In their *Risk and Insurance Management Manual for Libraries,* Mary Breighner, William Payton, and Jeanne M. Drewes identify six steps in the risk management process:[1]

1. Risk identification—Where are the risks? What could they be?
2. Risk quantification and evaluation—What will it cost to make your institution's buildings, collections, and staff members safe? What will it cost the institution if you have a loss of security?
3. Risk avoidance—How can your institution, security department, and staff avoid these risks?
4. Loss prevention and control—What remedial and proactive steps can you take to prevent and control loss of safety to staff and users, as well as the loss of collections?
5. Risk financing—How will you finance proactive steps, replacement of lost collections, and prevention of additional loss?
6. Reevaluation—How often will you reevaluate security and safety concerns and update your routines and training?

The *Risk and Insurance Management Manual for Libraries* provides a thorough discussion of risk management relevant to all cultural institutions and is highly recommended.[2] It focuses on aspects of risk management as they relate to the safety and security of the contents and users of cultural institutions.

The five major areas of risk or threat are

1. Internal and external security for the buildings, the people, and the collections
2. Physical damage and threats to the buildings and the collections themselves
3. Adverse weather and other natural phenomena that can cause damage to the buildings and injury to users and staff members
4. People, both users and staff, who might injure one another, themselves, or the collections
5. Technology, or rather, the loss of technology, both hardware and software

In the chapters that follow we will look at all of these threats, sometimes together, sometimes separately. It is essential to realize that security and safety work together and hence to consider them together. This book treats the topics separately, isolating each issue to facilitate discussion. Nevertheless, in the end they must be integrated and work as a whole.

While analyzing the risk of loss and damage to your collections and staff, consider the impact of each of the various threats upon the operational capabilities of the area. What would happen if a number of staff were unable to come to work due to illness or natural disaster? How would this affect the security of the collections and the quality of service? If part of the collections were damaged, could the institution continue to carry out its mission? Are there enough staff members to control access to the buildings and safeguard the collections when your institution is short-staffed?

There are other factors to consider as well. How vulnerable are the buildings and collections to theft and damage?[3] Where are the most vulnerable places? Does the library or archive have any control over these vulnerable areas? Is there a way to prevent losses and anticipate future threats to the integrity of the collections and the safety of users and staff members? Work with security personnel as well as facilities and maintenance staff to head off losses and develop your plan.

When considering risk, think about what that level of risk means to the survival of the institution or to particular departments or functions. Be realistic. It is impossible to plan for every risk. Try to work on the issues that provide the most protection for the most collections. The smaller issues will fall into place along the way.

Notes

1. Mary Breighner, William Payton, and Jeanne M. Drewes, *Risk and Insurance Management Manual for Libraries* (New York: Library Administration and Management Association, American Library Association, 2005), chapter 1.
2. For another perspective on risk management, see Alice Cannon, "Risk Management," in *Disaster Management for Libraries and Archives,* ed. Graham Matthews and John Feather (Aldershot, UK, and Burlington, VT: Ashgate, 2003).
3. See also René Teygeler, "Writing a Disaster Plan: Identifying Risk," in *Preparing for the Worst, Planning for the Best: Protecting Our Cultural Heritage from Disaster,* ed. Joanna G. Wellheiser and Nancy E. Gwinn (Munich: K. G. Saur, 2005), 138–39.

Part

1

BUILDING SECURITY

Chapter

1

Surveying Exteriors and Grounds

Exterior building security, also called premises security, encompasses the grounds and structures outside the institution proper as well as each building's entrances and exits.[1] Exterior security provides the first line of protection for collections, staff, and patrons alike. Unfortunately, in many cases it is also the most vulnerable line. Staff awareness of the facility's vulnerable spots is essential.

To evaluate your facility's exterior security, first obtain or draw basic building plans for each structure and every floor within the structure. You do not need "as built" blueprints. In fact, the floor plans you distribute to patrons to show where collections are located are likely suitable for this exercise, though you will need to add to these all the staff and nonpublic sections of the building. This exterior survey will be the first of several evaluations that use these floor plans, and you will be adding information to the plans each time. Make several copies of each floor plan, then combine the information onto a master plan when you are finished surveying the building. This will simplify the process. You will also want an overall institutional map if your institution has buildings scattered across a campus. You can use any map that shows the layout of the institution with all its buildings, pathways, and roads.

The overall institutional map will allow you to organize your various surveys by building or location. This overall institutional map becomes the key or guide for testing your security plan and also for your disaster response plan. Keep copies of the information in safe locations at the central security office, in administrative or departmental offices, with each security plan, and at home.

When considering the security of a building, institution, or campus, look at the building(s) as a whole and as separate parts. Design a building survey plan that is specific to each structure. Consider all the vulnerable points and problematic issues for your building. Place every item on a survey form. Examine each feature, inside and outside, and identify the strong and weak points of your building security. Mark them on your survey form and on your building plan. Finally, create a checklist for follow-up with any problems or maintenance issues you noted.

The remainder of this chapter consists of a generic survey of exterior building security. Be sure to modify this survey to fit your situation. Some of it is common sense, and some requires awareness on the part of security guards, buildings and grounds crews, or facilities and maintenance personnel.

SURVEY OF EXTERIOR BUILDING SECURITY

On a survey of the building exteriors and institution grounds, you are looking for vulnerable or dangerous areas. Look for places that are dark at night, where there is limited access or visibility, or that are just potential hazards. Repeat this survey at least twice a year, in the fall and after the last snowfall of the winter. If you have a lot of snow and ice in the winter, you might want to make some of this external building survey part of your weekly routine in coordination with the buildings and grounds department or the facilities and maintenance department, whichever is responsible for caring for the outside of the buildings.

For each building, indicate which of the following external features are present for that structure on your overall map of the institution.

Plantings

Start with the plantings around the exterior of the building. Are there bushes close to the building where a person could hide? You want to make certain that plantings are far enough away that there is a discrete distance between the building and bushes or hedges. Although hedges are sometimes described as layers of defense and are used to surround the perimeter of an institution instead of a fence, they can be used as a hiding place.

Bushes and hedges that grow taller than the windows obstruct the view, so no one can see inside or out. You want to prune the bushes and trees so they do not block the windows, doors, and stairwells. This is a definite hazard at night or on days with few staff on-site. Foundation plantings become home to birds and small rodents as well as numerous insects. Diligent landscaping will prevent these pests from entering the building.

Cutting back ground cover and climbing plants such as ivy will prevent them from attaching to the walls and growing up them. This will do two things: prevent intruders from using the plants to climb into or out of the building, and keep the physical structure intact. Plants growing on the outside of the building provide easy handholds to gain access to upper levels that may seem inaccessible. When plants climb up walls, they send roots or fingers into the mortar or under the siding, allowing the elements, particularly water, access. This can encourage birds and insects to nest, weakening the walls and bricks. Eventually water will get into the structure of the walls and cause the building structure to rot.

Beware of trees growing close to structures. Trees enable access to upper levels if there are low branches. Keep trees trimmed to prevent limbs from scraping against the building exterior. Trim branches so that none are below ten feet in order to prevent people from climbing into the building. In addition, pruning and trimming trees will keep them healthy and able to withstand most storms, and will thereby prevent branches and trunks from breaking during bad weather, damaging the exterior of the building, breaking windows, walls, or roofs, or even taking down power and phone lines. An interruption in power and telecommunications means buildings are vulnerable to thieves who could take computer and office equipment, artwork, and even cash that is present in offices. A backup generator is essential to power security systems that include building alarms, security lights, and even telecommunications.

Security staff should patrol and monitor the outside of the building, looking for people hiding between bushes and the building. This will discourage homeless people from living there. It will also prevent people from gaining access to the building through windows. The facilities and maintenance staff should watch for a buildup of debris or garbage, which can encourage animals and insects and may affect the quality of the air entering the building through the fresh-air intake grates.

Large grates, vents, and air shafts on roofs and at ground level should be wired with alarms. Security should check the area any time that windows are open. Alarm panels should indicate when the grates and vents are open or closed. Only authorized personnel should be working in and around the grates and vents. Grates that are left open permit unauthorized access to the building. In addition, they pose a fire and water hazard during inclement weather.

Windows

Walk around the building and look at the windows. Take your outside building plan and indicate where the windows are in relationship to the ground, to entrances and exits, and to external stairways. Are there large plate-glass windows in the building, or are they all smaller? Did the architect design the building so the windows open? What is the library or archive's policy concerning opening windows on hot days? Preservation standards recommend that windows be closed at all times to help maintain constant temperature and relative humidity and thereby increase the life span of collections.

Are the first floor windows accessible from the ground? That is, can you just open them and climb right in, or do you need to stand on a box or ladder to reach them? Windows that allow for easy first floor access should be locked at the end of the working day, if not all the time. The windows should have some type of alarm so that security knows if someone opens a window when the building is closed. If the windows are locked at all times, then the alarms should ring whenever anyone opens a window or breaks the glass. Security should physically and visually inspect first floor or ground-level windows to prevent unauthorized access through them.

Determine if there are windows below ground level. You are looking for a number of potential security problems, including open or broken windows. We all know that libraries and archives routinely locate historical and special collections in the basement or in below-ground levels. It is also common for access to these collections to be restricted. Thus an open window to a below-ground collection or storage area is of great concern. All below-ground windows should be locked after working hours, if not all the time. Alarms indicating open or broken windows in below-ground rooms should ring in the security area after hours, and those for areas that are strictly storage should ring at all hours. If the windows are locked at all times, then the alarms should notify security that there is unauthorized access to the below-ground collections and someone should visually and physically check to make certain all is secure.

Check to see if any windows that are more than ten feet above the ground are broken or open. Any above-ground windows that are accessible from an outside staircase should be locked. Do any windows open onto terraces or balconies? If so, there should be open-window and glass-breakage alarms affixed to the windows. There should be alarms on those windows, and the alarms should ring in the security area.

In inclement weather, all windows should be shut and locked. The facilities and maintenance department should keep a supply of plywood on hand for boarding up broken windows. Broken windows should be replaced as soon as possible.

External Stairs

Look at the exterior stairs, those that go to upper levels, and most particularly, those that go to below-ground entrances. Take your map or floor plan and indicate on it where the external stairways are located. Indicate which stairs go to upper floors and which go below ground level.

First, look to see if the stairs that lead below ground are well maintained. Are all the treads intact? If there are broken steps and treads, block off the area until they are repaired and have them fixed as soon as possible. Are debris or leaves lying on the steps and in the bottom of the stairwell? If so, have buildings and grounds personnel remove them. You want to keep the drains clear of all obstructions to prevent water from pooling and then coming in under the doorways, and thereby prevent water damage on the inside of the building. Check to see if the facilities and maintenance department or the buildings and grounds department has a maintenance or cleaning schedule for the stairwells. Who is responsible for this activity? How often do they clean?

Are the below-ground stairwells closed off in inclement winter weather? If so, who is responsible for doing this? Perhaps your institution routinely closes below-ground stairwells at the beginning of the winter. Regardless of whether the below-ground stairs are closed or open, determine which department is responsible for checking to see if leaves and debris or ice and snow are removed from the drains at the bottom of the stairwells. If an external company is responsible for cleaning and maintaining the outside of your buildings, does it take care of snow and ice on stairs? Collect the twenty-four-hour contact information for this company and put it in your plan.

Next, examine the above-ground stairs. Are they made of metal grating and used primarily as fire escapes? Are they attached to fire escapes that must be pulled down or lowered in the event of a fire? If so, have them checked regularly to ensure they will function when needed. Alternatively, are the stairs made of stone or concrete and used routinely? If so, are they intact and safe?

No matter what they are made of, you need to see if the above-ground stairs are maintained. Who is responsible for cleaning away leaves and debris or ice and snow in the winter months? Is there a drain at the bottom of these stairs? If so, is it covered with debris and leaves? Will someone slip on ice or in water using those stairs? Is there a way to close off the stairs that go to upper levels if the weather is inclement?

If the stairs are the kind you pull down when evacuating from a fire, how easy is it to lower the ladder? Is the ladder secured to prevent mischief and vandalism? Nevertheless, you need to make certain the ladder releases in case of an emergency.

If the stairs are made of stone or concrete, is there some kind of tread to keep people from slipping when the steps are wet? Are there ridges or rough strips at the edges of the steps to provide better traction? If so, check to see that they are in good shape and repair any broken or damaged strips. The same is true of handicapped-accessible ramps.

Look at the lighting around these stairs. Do the lights actually come on at dark, or when it is overcast? Do the lights illuminate the stairs from top to bottom, or just the entranceways? Is the lighting bright enough to prevent someone from falling down and injuring themselves? If there is a power outage, are the lights on battery backup or a generator?

Lastly, who actually uses these external stairways? Are they primarily used by staff to enter and exit the building after hours? Or are they used by everyone? Are the stairwells used as emergency exits for below-ground offices and reading areas? For the upper-level stairs, do the staff members who work in those departments know how to lower the fire escape ladders in case of emergency?

If these external stairways are used as emergency exits only, will physically handicapped people be able to use them? It is possible that the handicapped-accessible exits and ramps are not near the emergency exits. If so, work with the disaster response or safety committee and discuss how to evacuate patrons and staff members who are wheelchair-bound or who cannot use stairs.

Walkways and Ramps

While you are looking at all the stairways, take note of the walkways and ramps into and around the buildings. Do their paths correspond with those on your map? If not, draw in the walkways. Indicate where the ramps for handicapped-accessible entrance to the buildings are located.

Now look at the walkways and ramps themselves. Are they smooth or cracked and distorted? Do the walkways have strips or ridges to facilitate traction? Have tree roots pushed up the pavement? Perhaps the salt that is used to melt ice has eaten holes in the asphalt. If the paths are uneven, schedule maintenance work on the surfaces. This may be the responsibility of the buildings and grounds department or the facilities and maintenance department. Alternatively, the institution might arrange to contract out the work. Fixing the uneven pavement will make access to the buildings safer and easier for physically handicapped patrons as well as everyone else.

Examine the ramps; are they still level? Is the section where the ramp meets the flat pathway still flush with the surface of the sidewalk? Pavement can settle or buckle at these joints, making it difficult to get a wheelchair up onto the ramp, or off of it, for that matter. If the ramp has ridges or rough strips to provide traction, make certain they are in good repair. See if the strips are affixed to the ramp surfaces. If not, have the strips replaced.

Look at the curb cuts and curbs. Curb cuts are designed to allow access for maintenance vehicles, bicycles, and wheelchairs. Are these surfaces smooth or ridged for traction? Are they damaged in any way? Is it clearly indicated that the curb cuts are handicapped-accessible? Are the curbs damaged or crumbling? If the curbs and curb cuts are damaged, arrange for them to be repaired when the walkways are fixed.

Look out the exit doors. Can you see the ramps, curb cuts, and curbs clearly? Does the external lighting illuminate the walkways, ramps, and curbs? Is any of this external lighting connected to the generators so that these areas will be lit during a power outage? Test the lighting to see that it works when the power is out.

Walkways, ramps, and curb cuts should be cleared of ice and snow during inclement weather to prevent injury and permit safe access to the building.

Storm drains are often located under curbs. During the next heavy rain, make certain that the drains are not obstructed by leaves and debris. If the drains are blocked, the flat areas will flood, making walking and driving hazardous. Debris and leaves should not be swept into storm drains, but should be removed to appropriate containers or areas on the grounds.

Parking Areas

After you finish looking at the external stairways, walkways, and ramps, turn your attention to the parking areas. You are looking for parts of the parking areas that might be a safety or security hazard for both patrons and staff.

Start with surface parking lots that are near the library. Is there overhead lighting that illuminates the entire lot or just part of it? If the lighting illuminates only part of the lot, mark the areas on your map that are dark and indicate that they are potential safety hazards. Have the buildings and grounds department replace any broken light fixtures.

Indicate on your map and in your security plan what time the parking area lights come on at night. Indicate whether the lighting stays on all night or only for a short time after the library closes.

Continue to look at the parking area at night. Can you see all the cars? If not, does the library provide a security guard to walk patrons to their cars after dark? Create a policy for this, and be certain to have the circulation staff let patrons know the service is available.

Are there concrete dividers and curbs in the parking lot? They need to be cleared of debris in the spring and fall, of ice and snow in the winter, and after storms so that drivers can see the dividers and curbs. Just as the stairways, walkways, and ramps should be kept clean of debris, snow, and ice, so should the parking areas. Walking areas should be cleared after snowstorms. Entrances to the parking lots should be free of obstructions, allowing safe ingress and egress. Determine which department handles this maintenance job and indicate it in your plan.

Not all libraries and archives have flat parking lots. Many have parking ramps that either are attached to the building or are nearby. Look at these parking ramps.

With map in hand, walk around the parking ramp. How do patrons enter the building from the parking ramp? Is the ramp physically attached to the building? Is there access through a walkway or enclosed bridge? Perhaps patrons exit the ramp and cross a walkway or street to gain access to the building. All these areas need to be well lit and monitored in order to prevent injury to patrons and staff. Security should make the parking ramp part of their route.

Walk through the parking ramp and look for safety hazards. This is particularly important if the parking ramp is attached to the library or archive. Look for unlit or visually obstructed areas. Are all the levels and the parking slots of the parking ramp well lit? Make sure that the buildings and grounds department or the facilities and maintenance department replace burned-out light bulbs.

Are there stairways and elevators in the parking ramp? Indicate on your map which levels have handicapped access to the elevators. The facilities and maintenance department should check regularly to make certain that power-assisted doors work. The buildings and grounds department or the facilities and maintenance department should make sure that lights are working in all the stairways and the elevator areas of the parking ramp. Security should check these stairways and elevator areas prior to locking the parking ramp for the night.

Check the stairwells for debris and physical hazards. Make certain the doors are unobstructed and open easily. Is there an elevator? If so, check for debris and obstructions that make it hazardous to use the equipment.

Look for an emergency phone or intercom that dials the security desk. Where are these phones located? Typically, these security phones are placed near exits and stairwells or elevators for easy access. How quickly does the security department respond to calls? What types of questions do the security personnel ask when they answer the phone? How efficiently does the security department respond to emergency calls from the parking ramp? Does the security system tell the office where the caller is? The security phone should dial the police or fire department when the building is closed.

Examine the visual range of the security cameras in the parking ramp. How much of the area do the cameras capture? Do the cameras film continuously or are they motion-activated? Do the security cameras monitor the phones? Does the security department monitor these cameras? How long are the videotapes kept before they are reused? Create a recycling schedule of no less than two weeks for them. Tapes should be date- and time-stamped for continuity and in case they are needed for legal reasons.

If the parking structure is connected to a building, security should be able to close off access between the building and the parking structure during an emergency, a fire drill, and after hours.

Are there restricted hours for the parking ramp? Does the ramp open and close right around the hours of the library? What type of gate is used to close off the parking ramp? If it is just an arm, what prevents people from breaking into the ramp after hours? If the parking ramp is closed when the library is closed, are the lights turned off after hours? When do they go back on? Is the parking ramp closed by lowering a metal gate? Does the gate drop or open automatically when the power goes off? How do you open or close it if there is a power outage? Is there any policy in place for opening the gate after hours? If so, what is it?

Security should check the parking ramp for cars and packages left after closing. If the parking ramp is physically attached to the building, then all entranceways should be locked and alarms set when the building is secured for the night. Appropriate precautions should be taken to determine that no items (cars, bikes, motorcycles, or packages) left in the parking ramp after hours will damage the building, air-handling system, or patrons. The security department should contact the local fire and police departments if any suspicious objects are left in the parking ramp overnight.

Set up a meeting with the security department to discuss criteria for requesting the removal of potentially hazardous packages, and for checking vehicles left overnight for explosives and biological or chemical hazards. Discuss what constitutes a suspicious item and who should contact the security and police departments.

Indicate on your map where the emergency exit from the parking ramp is located. This emergency exit should be accessible during the day in case of emergency or fire. An alarm should ring and alert the security desk when this emergency exit is used.

External and Security Lighting

Personal safety is a key concern of libraries and archives. If we want people to come to our institutions after dark, then we must take pains to be certain the outside areas are well lit. Good lighting and visible security guards are just two ways to make patrons feel safe. In the same vein, libraries and archives need to foster a feeling of safety for their staff so they are willing to work after dark.

As you survey the exterior of the buildings and parking areas, look at the lighting. You need to look for three types of lighting: exterior-building lighting, parking area lighting, and walkway lighting. Indicate on your map where the lights are. Make note of any lights that are not functioning and have the facilities and maintenance department replace the bulbs. Set up a schedule to survey the after-dark lighting, alerting the security and facilities and maintenance departments or the buildings and grounds department when lights are not functioning.

External Building Lighting

Look at the exterior lighting first. These lights are attached to the building. Some activate if there is movement outside; these lights are useful if there is minimal foot traffic after dark. For instance, you might want motion-activated lights at your staff exit if it is in a separate location from the patron exit. The motion-activated lights should be on a timer for a long enough duration that staff can close the door, make certain it is securely locked, and walk down the walkway to the parking area. It is important to take into account the time it would take an older person or physically handicapped person to exit the building, or even someone with their hands full of bags, boxes, or books.

Other types of exterior lights are always on after dark. These lights illuminate all the exits and the walls of the building. Emergency exits should have an exterior light above their doorways. These could be motion-activated, but they must be on the battery backup or generator so they function in an emergency. Exterior lights are designed to reveal movement and activity outside the building. In this way, security staff are able to see who might be loitering outside the building at night and to spot malicious mischief. Most important, a well-lit building will encourage patrons to utilize the collection after normal working hours.

While looking at safety for our patrons, we do not want to forget the staff. Is the staff exit well lit at night? Must the staff walk through unlit areas to get to their vehicles? Nothing is worse than having well-lit exits for patrons, while making staff exit at night into a dark, deserted alley or back area.

Some of the exterior building lights should be on either the generator or battery backup in the event of a power failure. Set up a schedule to test the exterior emergency lighting with the department responsible for its maintenance and with the security department.

Parking Area Lighting

Good lighting in the parking areas and parking structures encourages patrons to use your collections after dark. No one wants to park in a dark place, walk through dimly lit walkways, and then enter the building. Poorly lit areas create places where people can lurk or hide.

There should be good lighting in the stairwells, elevators, and elevator lobbies of all parking structures. In fact, there should be good lighting throughout the parking structure. There should not be any unlit areas in the structure. Patrons and staff will feel safe if they walk into a well-lit parking garage in the evening. Have security guards report any dark areas during their rounds, and have maintenance or facilities personnel replace burned-out bulbs immediately.

Good lighting in parking lots is equally important. The lights should illuminate the entire lot, including staff parking areas. Some institutions have limited hours or are located near residential areas. These institutions may have to adhere to city or county ordinances that require the lights in the parking areas to be off after a certain hour. If this is the case, indicate in your safety plan what that time is. Does someone have to turn the lights off as part of the closing routine, or are the lights on a timer? Indicate this in your safety plan. At the same time, find out if the parking area lights are on a different electrical circuit than the library or archive building. If so, is there some type of backup for generating power to these lights?

Walkway Lighting

Just as parking areas and parking structures need to be well lit, so do the walkways going from these areas to the building. You want the lighting to extend from the parking area or structure all the way to the building entrance. The lighting should also illuminate the handicapped ramps, walkways from external and below-ground stairways, and paths from emergency and staff doors.

Survey the area after dark to see if the lights illuminate these walkways. Look to see if the lighting is close to the ground or overhead. Are there dark patches where the lighting does not intersect? If so, consider remedying the situation when you have funds for improvements.

Access to the Building

The outside building survey is almost complete, and there are just a few more items to look for. Find the access points into the buildings. In this post-9/11 environment, it is now the norm to have only one entrance and exit from the building. If there are separate exits, people can only go out of these doors and must reenter the building at a different point. In a great number of cases, this is true for patrons as well as staff.

So where is the entrance to your building? Is it above ground level? Today this is uncommon because of the required compliance with the Americans with Disabilities Act (ADA).[2] Buildings must have either ground-level entrances or ramps to the upper-level doors. If your institution has more than one public entrance, how do physically handicapped people find the ground-level door? Is this handicapped-accessible entrance on a different side of the building? Can you access it easily from the parking area or parking structure? Are there signs indicating where the handicapped-accessible entrance is? Mark this information on your map.

If your library or archive is accessed through an above-ground entrance, how accessible is it during inclement weather? Do you close the upper-level entrance and make everyone come through the ground-level door? Can you change the directional signs to let the public know this before they park?

Do staff members enter the library through a separate entrance? If so, how is this access point controlled? Does the entrance require key cards, keys, or an intercom system? If there is an intercom, can the person see who is outside prior to releasing the door lock? Indicate this in your safety plan. Consider other ways you can protect your staff while entering and exiting after hours.

Emergency Exits—from the Outside

Walk around the building with your map in hand. Identify on your map where the emergency exits are. All the emergency exit doors should have a push bar that opens and then locks upon exiting the building. These external doors should never be propped open. There should be key access from the outside, especially if there is no door handle. Indicate on your map whether the doors open at ground level, above, or below. You will want to see if the emergency exits open onto walkways or stairways. If they do, is it possible to open these doors from the outside? In other words, are there handles on the outside of the doors? If there is only a key lock, would you have to pull the door open with the key?

If the emergency doors open onto walkways and stairways, then add some directional arrows to the map indicating which direction people move away from the building and the parking structures. This will be important if there is a fire or bomb threat in the building and you need to evacuate. Identify a safe location away from the building where staff can gather. Mark it on your map and in your security plan. If possible, use the same gathering place as in the disaster response plan. Make certain that this location is handicapped-accessible and that all staff members know where it is. At this safe location, collect all the names of staff members who evacuated the building. This will ensure that you can identify who might be missing and trapped in the building. This list will also serve to let the administration know who was sent home or relocated in the event of the disaster or emergency.

When using the emergency exits, staff members should direct patrons to safe areas that provide a gathering place away from buildings and parking areas. Mark these safe areas for evacuating patrons on the map. Use arrows to show how to get to the safe areas. Make certain the area is handicapped-accessible. Be certain the map has a "YOU ARE HERE" label along with a north-pointing arrow for quick orientation.

Some emergency exits open onto grassy areas. Indicate which path staff and patrons should use to evacuate, and mark the safe gathering place on the map.

If only some of the exits are handicapped-accessible, staff should be aware of these specific locations. If none of the emergency exits is handicapped-accessible, then discuss with administration and security how you will evacuate these patrons in case of an emergency. Coordinate this part of the plan with the disaster response team, security, and the fire department.

While you are looking at the emergency exits, take note of any obstructions outside the doors and on the walkways and stairways. Have the buildings and grounds department clear away debris and plantings in order to keep the emergency exits ready for evacuation.

Loading Docks

The final areas to look at in our external building survey are the loading dock and the access to the freight elevator that opens onto the loading dock area. Loading dock doors should be locked at all times when not in use to discourage unauthorized entrance to the building.

Who accesses the building through the loading dock? Is there a security guard at the loading dock who alerts the staff that there is a delivery, or is there a phone or buzzer system? If the loading dock door requires a key, then list the people who have copies. If the door requires a key code or key card, how is access limited to this entrance, and are there any restrictions on the times this door is used? Set up a procedure to check out the loading dock key for those staff members who need it irregularly.

What is the protocol for accessing the building through the loading dock? If there are security guards, are they responsible for directing the driver to the location within the building, or is a staff member required to accept the delivery at the loading dock? If there are no security guards, then how does the driver alert the library or archive staff that there is a delivery? Is there a phone or buzzer outside the loading dock doors? Place a sign above the phone giving department numbers for the shipping or mail room or the acquisitions department, or perhaps even the circulation desk. If there is only a buzzer, then who is responsible for answering it? If the door-release mechanism is released from a reception desk inside the building, how will you identify who is outside?

Is there a camera or security device that records or shows people at the loading dock? Whoever is using the loading dock door for deliveries should be accompanied at all times. Create a procedure for handling the delivery of materials and supplies at the loading dock and put it in the safety plan.

If the freight elevator opens to the outside of the building in the loading dock, how is access to it restricted? A key, key code, or key card should open this elevator door. Discuss with the administration who has access and document those people or departments. Security, shipping, and the facilities and maintenance department probably require access to the loading dock, as well as the acquisitions and circulation departments. Keep the key in a central location for those staff members who need the key on an irregular basis.

Survey the loading dock, looking at the lighting. Is the light connected to a motion-activated sensor, so the light goes on when a vehicle pulls up into the area? If so, then set the light's timer for the average time a delivery takes. Loading dock lights that are not connected to a motion sensor should illuminate the area completely during all hours the building is open. Some of the lights should be on either battery backup or the generator so the area is lit when there is a power failure.

For health reasons, trucks should not be allowed to idle in the loading dock, especially if there is a fresh-air intake in the area. Carbon monoxide will build up in the loading dock area and enter the air-handling system. The results can range from discomfort to a severe health risk, depending on the configuration of the loading dock and the location of the fresh-air intake.[3]

One more item to document about the loading dock is its orientation to the building. Do vehicles drive into a covered area to get to the loading dock, or is there no protective covering above the dock? Is the loading dock flush with the ground, or below or above grade? Perhaps there is a platform that the truck backs into that allows the delivery to be carted directly from the bed of the truck into the building. Does the light illuminate the stairs to the side of this above-ground loading dock?

The loading dock area should be monitored during inclement weather. All debris, ice, and snow should be removed on a regular basis, ensuring that all drains run freely. Clearing away debris, snow, and ice from the stairs at the side of the dock is imperative in inclement weather to prevent injury.

If the loading dock is accessed through a covered area, is there a way to lock off the dock when it is not in use? The loading dock doors or gates should be secured at ground level. Check to see that the mechanical release for the loading dock doors is in good working order so it will function during a power failure.

Now that we have surveyed the outside of the building, we will proceed to the inside of the building. Go to the main entrance and begin the next set of surveys there.

Notes

1. Interior building security will be covered in chapter 2.
2. Americans with Disabilities Act, *Code of Federal Regulations,* title 36, chap. 11, pts. 1191–1194.
3. Indoor air quality is beyond the scope of this book. For more information on indoor air quality issues in cultural institutions, see U.S. Environmental Protection Agency and U.S. Department of Health and Human Services, *Building Air Quality: A Guide for Building Owners and Facility Managers* (Washington, DC: Government Printing Office, 1991), available at http://www.cdc.gov/niosh/baqtoc.html; J. Tétreault, *Airborne Pollutants in Museums, Galleries, and Archives: Risk Assessment, Control Strategies, and Preservation Management* (Ottawa: Canadian Conservation Institute, 2003); and Garry Thomson, *The Museum Environment,* 2nd ed. (London and Boston: Butterworths, 1986).

Chapter

2 Surveying Interior Public Areas

Before beginning your interior survey, you will need to have or create a floor plan for every level of each building that houses library and archival materials at your institution and any floors that have the mechanical equipment (air-handling systems, boiler, etc.) that serves those areas. These can be the simple floor plans that you give to students and visitors showing them where each department is. Supplement these plans with information about the "staff" or nonpublic areas. You do not need anything as formal as blueprints or "as built" plans.

Walk through each floor of the building just as you would when creating a disaster response plan. In addition to looking for recurring maintenance and water problems, look at security and potential safety issues. Some basic questions to ask are

1. Is the entire floor visible from either the reference/information desk or the elevator/stairway?
2. Can you see the emergency exit from the stairs or elevator area? Can you see the signs?
3. Can patrons enter staff areas without being noticed?

Create a checklist to follow up on any changes or problems noted during your internal building survey.

ENTRANCES AND EXITS

In today's security-conscious atmosphere, there should be only one exit and one entrance to the building, preferably at the same place.[1] Meeting rooms that are outside the library proper should have an exit door that automatically locks upon leaving, especially after hours. Although the meeting rooms may have access to restrooms, the rest of the library should be locked off when the building is closed for the day.

When patrons and staff enter, security staff should examine entrants' belongings as a safety measure for those within the building. They should look for weapons or devices that could cause harm. When patrons and staff exit, security staff should examine their belongings as a security for the integrity of the collections. They should look for materials that belong to the library or archive that have not been properly checked out or that have been removed from noncirculating collections. (See the checklist "General Collections: Entrances" in appendix A.)

Start with the public entrance. Since September 11, 2001, many large institutions monitor all entrances with security guards and/or security machines. All staff, visitors, patrons, and service personnel enter through these security gates and send all their belongings through the security machines. Instruct all security staff that everyone must follow these safety rules, with no exceptions. Post policies and procedures for all to read, and distribute copies of the policies upon request.[2]

Exit doors can be at the same location or in a different place. There should be no way to reenter the building through the exit doors for either staff or patrons. Secondary entrances and exits to the building should be secured with alarms and used as emergency exits only. Post signs to direct users to the appropriate exit.

If there are security devices for scanning staff and patrons and their belongings, these stations should be staffed during all hours the building is open. You might consider limiting the hours that staff can enter and exit the building, or create a different security scanning procedure for after-hours access to the building.

Security staff should check all parcels and persons as they leave the building to confirm that books and other collections have been checked out at the circulation desks or checkout machines. All staff should be reminded not to remove circulating materials from the collections without checking them out. All noncirculating materials must remain in the building. If an exception is made, then temporary circulation records should be created so that the location of these materials can be tracked. (There is more information on this in chapter 4, "Security for General Collections.")

If the library has no guards, someone should still monitor who and what is leaving the building. This responsibility often falls to the circulation staff, who should be alert to security alarms ringing, either at the regular exit or the emergency exit doors. Any time an emergency exit alarm rings, someone should be assigned to determine why it rang, who left, and what was removed through that door. (See the checklist "General Collections: Exits" in appendix A.)

CONCEALED WEAPONS

If your state permits individuals to carry concealed weapons—and most states do—then the institution should post signs at all entrances prohibiting weapons. Most states with "concealed carry laws" prohibit the carrying of weapons onto the grounds of cultural institutions, libraries, universities, and colleges. Nevertheless, your institution should post signs to remind people that it is illegal to carry a concealed weapon on the grounds. Security guards must enforce this prohibition. Some public institutions have a secure location in which to lock firearms and other weapons until the owner leaves. If yours does not, then ask patrons to secure weapons in their vehicles before entering the building.

Check your state's law code to determine the exact wording on the signs prohibiting concealed weapons. If you have any questions about this issue, contact your legal counsel and local law enforcement agency.[3]

CIRCULATION DESKS AND CHECKOUT MACHINES

There is usually a circulation desk or an information desk as patrons enter the library or archive proper. The circulation desk may have a security device to monitor the unauthorized removal of items from the collection. The security system may ring or it may close when materials leave without being desensitized at the circulation desk. Security staff should monitor this area and direct patrons back to the circulation desk to check out materials. If there is no security staff at this location, then circulation staff should ask patrons to return to the desk to check out items.

Establish procedures for staff to follow if patrons leave without checking out materials. Test the procedures to confirm that they do not endanger the safety of staff members. Such procedures may include the following:

1. Notify security staff immediately via the intercom or buzzer system to look for a specific individual during their exit check.
2. Document who took the materials if the patron's identity is known.
3. Ask security to review the videotape for that particular time to try to identify who took the items out of the building. These tapes should not be reused but saved as evidence of the theft.

4. Call the police to report the theft and the circumstances surrounding it.

LOCKER AREAS

In this same circulation or public entrance area, there may be lockers for patrons to use to store their belongings while using the library or archive. If it is a standing policy that all patrons store their belongings (coats, briefcases, backpacks, purses, personal books, etc.), then direct every person entering the building to this area first. Decide upon a maximum allowable size for a change purse or other personal items for people who want to bring in their valuables. Post this information on your website as a FAQ and in a prominent section about using your collections. This information will be particularly important for out-of-town and infrequent visitors. If restrictions on personal items apply only to special collections, rare books, and archives, then post the information on their section of the website in their FAQs.

If the locker area is not visible from the security or circulation desks, make certain there are security cameras or mirrors to monitor the room. The lockers should be secure enough that patrons will not hesitate to use them to store all their belongings. These monitoring devices enhance patrons' perception of safety.

Establish a policy for lost locker keys. Of course, you should have duplicates or passkeys so security can open the lockers at the end of the day or in an emergency. But what will your policy be if a patron loses his or her key? Will you return the items to the patron the next day or upon proof of ownership? Will you hold the items in the security office or lost and found to be surrendered upon proof of ownership? What if the patron cannot get home without the ID, keys, and money in the locker? Work with the security department to establish fair guidelines that will protect patrons' belongings from theft and at the same time preserve excellent customer relations.

CELL PHONES AND PAGERS

The institution's management will have to decide how or where to restrict cell phone use when patrons are using the collections and when they are in the building. Policies vary from institution to institution, just as the use of Walkman players, iPods, and other digital audio players within the building does. Some institutions ask that pagers and cell phones be placed on vibrate when in the building, while others prohibit them entirely. Many libraries and archives have a "cell phone zone." It is certainly acceptable to ask patrons to go outside or into the lobby if their cell phone conversations become disruptive to other patrons.

PERSONAL ITEMS (COMPUTERS, WRITING IMPLEMENTS, ETC.)

Post policies both on the website and in the building to indicate what patrons may bring into the library or archive. This is especially important for special collections. Many permit only plain paper and pencils. Make these items available for patrons to use.

Does your institution permit the use of laptop computers, digital cameras, PDAs, scanners, and other electronic devices in the library or archive?[4] Post this information, permitting or prohibiting such devices, on your website. Establish a registration procedure for all electronic, computer, and digital equipment. Security staff must enforce these procedures and register all equipment coming in and going out of the building.[5]

Is there a different policy as to what people may bring into meeting rooms when people attend meetings or seminars at your library? Then remind the security staff of it on the day of the conference. It is also a good idea to let the meeting and seminar organizers know what attendees are permitted to bring with them, especially if the meeting or seminar room is located inside the collections area. We will take another look at meeting rooms and their associated safety and security issues near the end of this chapter.

EMERGENCY EXITS

Walk around the perimeter of each floor. Indicate on your map the location of each emergency exit. Confirm that there is easy access to each emergency door and that each sign is visible. There should not be equipment or furniture blocking the doorway. Doors should not be propped open (a fire code violation as well as a security risk). Do not bolt or lock the doors. An alarm should ring when the door is opened. Test the doors to make certain the alarm does go off. Coordinate this activity with the security department so they can determine which alarms ring where and can identify which doors have been opened. (There is more information on alarms in the next subsection.)

A lighted emergency exit sign should be posted above each emergency exit door. If there are emergency lights affixed to the exit sign, test them to make certain the battery backup works.

Since September 11, 2001, some institutions have placed emergency exit signs at floor level as well, so evacuees can find the exits if there is smoke in the building. These same institutions have painted stair treads and baseboards with fluorescent paint so people can find their way out in the dark or if there is smoke.

While examining all the emergency exits, open each door to determine whether it opens directly to the outside, into a corridor, or into a stairwell. If the door opens directly to the outside, make certain nothing prevents the door from opening. If the door opens into a corridor, make certain there are no boxes, shelves, or other items stored in the corridor (a fire code violation). Make certain the door at the other end of the corridor opens to the outside and that there is no difficulty opening it. If the emergency exit opens onto a landing in a stairwell, post signs at eye and floor level that indicate which direction (up or down) is out. Confirm that there are no items stored in the stairwell and on the landings. Place a sign on each emergency door that leads to the outside indicating where to gather when evacuating the building.

If there are emergency exits that are not handicapped-accessible, indicate these on your map. Post signs on those exits that are handicapped-accessible so patrons with limited mobility can both find them and make use of them.

Return to the main entrance to the floor and look to see if the emergency exits are visible from this central location. Also look at the floor from the central elevator or stairwell. If the emergency exits are not visible from there, indicate which ones are not visible on your follow-up checklist and your map. Post signs directing people to the nearest exit.

Take a look at the floor layout/emergency exit map posted next to the central elevator and stairwell on each floor. Does it indicate where the closest exit routes are located? Does the information on this map coincide with the floor plan in your hand? Does the orientation of the map make sense, and does it indicate "you are here"? Are the handicapped-accessible exits clearly indicated on both maps? If not, note which ones are not on your checklist and follow up on the changes.

ALARMS

Take a second look at the alarms. Many institutions have a number of security devices, including alarms. These alarms ring in the building to alert its occupants to a fire, smoke, or excess heat. A secondary alarm should ring at the campus security desk and at the community's public safety departments (police and fire). Other alarms include emergency exit door alarms, mechanical equipment alarms such as those on activated sump pumps, water alarms, broken glass alarms, and staff safety alarms. (This last type of alarm will be discussed in chapter 10.)

Emergency exit doors should have alarms that ring both at that location and at a security desk or a campus security office. Emergency alarms for fire or evacuation should be noted on your floor plan. ADA codes require emergency alarms that flash or strobe, as well as ring, in order to alert people with impaired hearing to the danger. Schedule a test to check that

1. All the alarms ring
2. The alarms can be heard and seen throughout the entire floor
3. The alarms can be heard and seen in all staff, closed stacks, and storage areas

In addition, exit door alarms indicate unauthorized ingress or egress from the building. They might also indicate that someone is using the door to remove objects from the building, be it furniture, equipment, or collections. The only reason the emergency exit alarms should ring is to permit occupants to leave in case of fire or evacuation. Security should respond to and investigate any unauthorized use of emergency exits. Discuss response time and procedures with the security department staff.

If equipment or furniture must be removed using emergency exits, notify the security department. Either security staff or library/archive staff members should be present during this process, especially when working with outside contractors.

Some mechanical equipment is wired into alarm and security systems. This equipment includes heating, ventilating, and air-conditioning (HVAC) systems, boilers, water heaters, and sprinkler systems. The rooms where mechanical equipment is housed should have fire and smoke detectors as well as water alarms. These alarms should all be wired into the central security system and have battery backup systems that activate during power outages. An alarm should ring at the security desk or the facilities and maintenance department alerting them that the power is out or that there is an equipment failure.

Talk to the security department to learn how they know which alarms indicate what is happening in your building. Set up routines and procedures for notifying the library or archive's disaster response team or security team, depending on which alarms ring. The campus- or institution-wide security and safety office, which may be called the safety department, works in conjunction with public safety departments in the community. If the campus security or safety office is not staffed twenty-four hours a day, then appropriate alarms should ring at the community's public safety building. This is crucial in the case of fire alarms. If they ring only in the building or on campus, then no one will know if there is a fire or any other problem after hours until it is too late.

MOTION DETECTORS AND CAMERAS

As a security measure, your institution might consider installing motion detectors or alarms at the building entrances of loading docks, mechanical rooms, and storage facilities. Indicate on your floor plan the entrances to private or staff areas where patrons could enter undetected. These same areas could be equipped with security cameras as well as motion detectors. Triggering the motion detector will notify security of any unauthorized entrance or activity. These detectors can be activated after hours or be active twenty-four hours a day. Motion detectors should be wired into the security system as all other alarm systems are. Again, security staff should respond to and investigate any unauthorized access to these nonpublic areas, especially after hours.

Look to see if there are security cameras covering the emergency exits. If so, who monitors activity near the doorways? Does the security staff know where each emergency exit is? Do the cameras automatically activate and begin to record if the emergency doors are opened and the alarm sounds?

SMOKE DETECTORS

Just as you indicated on the floor plan where the emergency exits are, do the same for fire alarms and fire extinguishers throughout the building.

Install detectors that monitor the presence of smoke, particulate matter, and excess heat throughout the library or archive in public and nonpublic areas. Note the location of these detectors on your floor plan and compare them with the information in your library's disaster response plan.

Smoke detectors are particularly important if there is no sprinkler system in the institution. Identify the smoke detectors in your disaster response plan and your floor plan. They provide safety for your staff and patrons as well as security for your collections. The smoke detectors should be wired into the main security system and into a backup generator in case of power failure.[6]

EMERGENCY LIGHTING

While surveying each floor, take a look at the emergency lighting. Not only should there be emergency lights affixed to the emergency exit signs, but they should also be above stairwell doors, in stairwells, and in internal corridors.

Is there emergency lighting in the restrooms and storage areas? If not, then have some installed. Place flashlights at reference and circulation desks and in other locations, including storage areas, where staff can reach them easily.

Test the emergency lights to make certain they go on when the power goes off. Indicate on your floor plan where the emergency lights are. If there are areas they do not illuminate, discuss this with the facilities and maintenance department or the security and safety department to see what can be done to install more emergency lighting.

HANDICAPPED EVACUATION

When we surveyed the outside of the building, we looked at where handicapped access ramps were located, and we mentioned that there should be signs indicating where those entrances are located. We also discussed indicating where handicapped-accessible emergency exits are. In this same vein, discuss with the institution's security and safety department how handicapped patrons and staff will be evacuated from the buildings in case of an emergency. These procedures should be present in your building's disaster response plan. Review the procedures and discuss which procedures need to be revised or updated.

If there are many stairwells or many floors in your building, you might consider purchasing a device to assist emergency personnel in evacuating wheelchair-bound staff and patrons down or up stairs. There are a number of companies that sell these devices.[7]

Indicate on your floor plan where the handicapped-accessible emergency exits are, if there are any internal ramps that connect departments or floors, and where the handicapped-accessible restrooms, meeting rooms, and study areas are located.

If you plan to modify the building at all to provide any of these safety measures while complying with the Americans with Disabilities Act, be certain to look at the ADA Accessibility Guidelines for Buildings and Facilities (ADAAG).[8]

MIRRORS

Convex mirrors in libraries serve a number of functions. The mirrors chiefly serve to provide views of obstructed stacks areas. Position the mirrors so staff at the reference and circulation desks can see into stacks that end at walls or are out of the line of sight of roving staff. This is particularly important in areas that serve children and young adults. If there is no line of sight across a floor, then staff and security must either walk the area to make certain all are safe and behaving properly, or there must be a way to see into those invisible corners. Mirrors work well, and so do security cameras. No matter which approach your institution selects, the staff must be vigilant and conscious of what is happening outside their immediate work area.

The mirrors also provide a way to confirm that staff members are safe from harm when helping patrons find items in the collections, especially when working in out-of-the-way stacks areas. In addition, mirrors provide a view of patron activities, discouraging stalking, exposing oneself, and malicious mischief.

Walk around the floor to determine what staff members see in the mirrors when seated or standing at reference and circulation desks. Check to see if the mirrors provide views of the main elevator and stairways. Indicate on your floor plan what is visible from which mirrors.

WINDOWS

If windows open, they must be locked at night and in inclement weather. You want to prevent unauthorized and unwanted entrance through the windows at all times. Open windows can be easy exits for patrons who don't wish to check out materials. As we discussed in chapter 1, open windows also encourage theft and unauthorized entrance after hours. If you must open windows, open them from the top. Of course, opening windows means that you change the environment in the building. This will allow fluctuations in temperature and relative humidity, provide access to insects and birds, and allow rain and snow inside. If at all possible, you will want to keep windows shut and locked. Library or archive staff and security staff should check the building at closing time to confirm that all windows are locked prior to turning on the alarm system.

If the building has an alarm system, then the windows should have alarms installed to report or indicate breakage and unauthorized opening. Windows that are below grade level, at ground level, and one floor above ground level should have alarms installed. All windows that open onto a roof or terrace area should also have alarms. Those that exit onto an external stairwell or fire escape should have an alarm and emergency release mechanism that opens the bars or gates. This means that every window that someone could just climb through without much trouble should be locked when no one is in the room, when the building is closed, or during inclement weather. The alarm system should indicate which windows and doors are open. Consult a security expert to determine which windows and doors need what types of alarms.

EMERGENCY PHONES

While walking around the interior of each building, look for emergency phones. They should be located near emergency exits or at stairwells. Use these phones to provide emergency access to fire, police, and security personnel at the institution and in the community when the building is closed. Such a phone could be the one in the elevator that calls security. Consider an additional phone somewhere on each floor in case the elevator is not working.

You need to have a few phones that do not require electricity or computers. Install a "regular" phone on each floor, in both public and staff areas.

Post signs on each floor indicating the presence of these emergency phones, and mark their locations on your floor plan.

MEETING ROOMS IN PUBLIC AREAS

Meeting rooms in and of themselves raise a variety of issues for cultural institutions, especially rooms that are outside the library or archive proper and yet are part of the building. These meeting rooms are used by both the library staff and the public for a variety of functions. They often have a kitchen area where food can be heated up and stored. Those that are outside the library proper often have doors that open to the outside of the building that bypass security. This means that the room can be used after the collections are closed for the day. These meeting rooms are usually in the atrium of the library or archive, and in many cases in the same area where there are public restrooms.

For safety's sake, your security guards should remain on the premises until the after-hours meetings are over. In this way, a representative of the institution is there to make certain everyone leaves and gets to their cars and buses. It also means that if there is an accident or an incident, there is someone from the institution to call for help and report the incident. When the last person leaves, security should check that the kitchen area is closed and all appliances are off. They should also check that the restrooms are empty and that the outside door is closed and locked.

Have security check the parking area to make certain everyone's car started and there is no one waiting for a ride home. If the parking lot lights are turned off manually at the end of the day, do so after the last person has exited the building. If the lights are on a timer, make certain they go off later than the last meeting would get out.

In addition to these external meeting rooms, there are usually meeting rooms inside the library or archive proper that may be used by the public or for related library or archive functions. Meetings and seminars in these rooms should end before the building closes for the day. Staff members and security guards should make certain everyone has left the room and that all audiovisual and computer equipment, if there is any, is still there and is properly secured.

Every once in a while there is an official function in the library or archive after the building is closed. In this case, it is imperative that there be security guards present to protect both the attendees and the collections. The security guards should also monitor the actions and movements of the caterers and any other contracted service people while they are in the building. The visitors should not have access to the nonpublic areas of the building. The security staff should be the last to leave the building after checking the public, staff, and collections areas and securing the building. Again, they should check that the parking areas are empty and that there is no one waiting for a ride home.

EVACUATION DRILLS AND SAFE ZONES

There are two types of drills: an evacuation drill, for which staff and patrons actually leave the building, due to fire or bomb threats; and an inclement weather drill, for which staff and patrons gather in safety zones inside the building. Make it a policy to practice each of these drills at least once a year.

For an evacuation drill, there should be a designated exterior location at which to gather, determine that all staff members who came to work have evacuated the building, and wait until you are directed by fire and safety personnel that it is safe to return to the building. Select an alternative location that is a few blocks away and is out of the elements in case of inclement weather. Never reenter a building to search for missing staff members. Instead, tell the fire and safety personnel that they are missing.

Drills for inclement weather are usually for tornadoes or hurricanes, although sometimes they are for mud slides, snowstorms, earthquakes, or floods. In these cases, work with the fire department to determine the safest place inside the building. Libraries, archives, historical societies, and museums should have a designated safety zone or shelter for evacuation during a tornado or hurricane when the institution is open. Unless directed, do not go outside during weather emergencies.

During drills, all patrons and staff should report either to the designated area outside or to the safe zone within the building. Work with the security department to designate a specific individual and an alternate to notify people when it is safe to return to the building proper.

If you must evacuate to stairwells because of the nature of your building, be certain that you have discussed this option with both the security department at your institution and the fire and safety departments in your community. Use your common sense about walking down multiple flights of stairs. Do not attempt to take handicapped or wheelchair-bound persons down multiple flights of stairs unless you are trained to do so. Have them wait for the fire and safety personnel responding to your disaster or security problem.

As we learned on September 11, 2001, stairwells can become unsafe. If the situation warrants, descend the stairs and exit the building. This has not been standard operating procedure in the past; during a fire, people were directed to remain in stairwells two or three floors below their working floor until the fire department directed personnel to evacuate (often by elevator). Fire safety procedures now require everyone to evacuate the building during a real emergency.

During your annual evacuation drill, test the alarm system to make certain that it is audible throughout all the public areas of the building, including the restrooms and study rooms. Test to determine that you can hear and see emergency announcements and alarms in all back rooms, offices, kitchens, lounges, and staff restrooms. Don't forget to check the audibility and visibility of alarms in storage areas, mechanical equipment rooms, and basements. If you cannot hear or see the alarms, your staff and patrons won't be able to hear or see them either.

If there is an emergency that requires closing the building or institution due to bad weather, think about the safety of any personnel or patrons who might become trapped in the building or are unable to go home. You might keep a small supply of potable water and nonperishable food, blankets, and flashlights in a storage closet or kitchen area. Let the staff know where these emergency supplies are. This can be part of your safety and disaster response planning effort. Be certain to replenish the supplies if they are used.[9]

REVIEW AND DOCUMENTATION

At the end of your survey of the inside of the building, check your floor plans to make certain you have identified the location of the emergency exits, alarms, security devices, and potential security issues. Document items to follow up and set a short time frame of no more than two months to accomplish the tasks.

Security and maintenance staff and members of the security and disaster response teams should have copies of these floor plans. Keep a copy with all emergency planning documents, and have copies available for distribution to emergency personnel when and if an emergency occurs. The fire department may ask for copies of your basic floor plans. Make certain that any "mystery" rooms (those without identifying signs) in staff and storage areas are labeled on these plans.

Notes

1. William E. Chadwick, "Special Collections Library Security: An Internal Audit Perspective," *Journal of Library Administration* 25, no. 1 (1998): 24–25.

2. For good examples, see the National Archives and Records Administration's policies (http://www.archives.gov/research/start/nara-regulations.html) and the Library of Congress's policy (http://www.loc.gov/rr/security).
3. An example of Ohio's requirements for posting signs and sources for signs is available at http://www.corsa.org/Default.aspx?tabid=83. Each state has regulations about where to post the signs in public and private buildings and what language and law codes to cite. Check with your legal counsel for more information.
4. Diane Kaplan, "Digital Cameras in Reading Rooms," *Archival Outlook,* March/April 2006, 6–7, 25, available at http://www.archivists.org/periodicals/ao_backissues/AO-Mar06.pdf.
5. The Library of Congress's policy can be found at http://www.loc.gov/rr/main/inforeas/portable.html, and the policies for the National Archives are found at http://www.archives.gov/research/.
6. For more information on this topic, consult Miriam B. Kahn, *Disaster Response and Planning for Libraries,* 2nd ed. (Chicago: American Library Association, 2002), and other books on disaster response. For assistance with assessing and designing security, see Layne Consultants International (http://www.layneconsultants.com) or Rothstein Associates Inc. (http://www.rothstein.com).
7. Lifeslider (http://www.lifeslider.com), Evac-Trac by Garaventa (http://www.garaventa.ca/index.html), and Pollock Lifts (http://www.pollocklifts.co.uk) are three companies that make devices to move wheelchair-bound people down stairs.
8. Section 8 of the ADAAG is concerned specifically with libraries and is available at http://www.access-board.gov/adaag/html/adaag.htm#lib.
9. Pamela Cravey, *Protecting Library Staff, Users, Collections, and Facilities: A How-to-Do-It Manual for Librarians* (New York: Neal-Schuman, 2001), 58–63.

Chapter 3

Surveying Staff-Only Areas

Staff-only areas are the areas of cultural institutions that are closed to the public or that are restricted-access-only areas, such as special collections, storage areas, and mechanical equipment rooms. This chapter focuses on safety issues for staff who work in these areas.

STAFF ENTRANCES AND EXITS TO THE BUILDING

Begin this part of the building survey by looking at how staff members enter those parts of the library or archive that are not open to the public. Is there a specific entrance to the building from the outside? Since September 11, 2001, many of these entrances have been closed off and staff members are now required to enter through public entrances. If this is not the case in your facility, should such a change be considered?

If staff members enter through a designated staff-only entrance, determine how they gain access to the building and how security is enforced at this door. Is there a key card system, a security keypad, or a guard who checks staff member identification cards when people enter and leave the building? Are there cameras to record entrances and exits? If the staff entrance has no security personnel, note this as a potential risk to the collections and weigh the risk against the cost of retaining security personnel.

Is this entrance staffed when the building is closed to the public? If not, how do staff members gain access after hours? Establish a policy for after-hours access as well as descriptions of exceptions to the policy, such as access during emergencies. This policy should already be part of your disaster response plan. Talk to the disaster response plan team leader to learn who is contacted in an emergency and how they plan to get access to the building.

If there are security personnel at the staff entrances, what do they check? Are staff members required to pass through metal detectors and X-ray screening machines? Do the security guards just look at staff badges, or do they look through packages and bags as well? Determine if security personnel check employees on the way out of the building to see if employees are removing materials without checking them out first.

If there are key cards and electronic keypads for accessing staff entrances or staff-only interior spaces, what is the protocol for changing the system when staff members resign or are fired? The security department as well as the security staff assigned to your buildings should be informed of these personnel changes immediately. Traditionally, access to staff areas of the buildings and collections is revoked after resigning employees exit the building on their last day. In some institutions, staff members who resign or are fired are escorted to their offices by security personnel, who confirm that only personal items are removed from the building. At the same time, the former employee's access to staff areas is permanently revoked, and security is alerted to the change in personnel and key codes. The same holds true for computer passwords, intranet access, voice mail, and e-mail accounts, as well as access to circulation records. When employees depart, human resources personnel should collect their ID badges and any special keys or key cards that provide employee-level access to buildings and collections.

STAFF AREAS AND OTHER NONPUBLIC AREAS OF THE BUILDING

Staff areas and restricted-access areas are those parts of the building not normally seen by the public. There will be times when consultants, visitors, contractors, and professional colleagues will come to these areas, but this is not the norm. Staff areas include administrative and staff offices, workrooms, storage areas, mechanical rooms, and staff conference rooms, lounges, kitchens, and cafeterias. Restricted-access areas include restricted or locked storage areas for rare books, special collections, unprocessed archives and artwork, computer server rooms, electrical closets, and the like. If your institution is a closed stacks library, then only employees should have access to the areas where books and other media are shelved. Even in a closed stacks facility, however, rare and valuable materials should still be stored in restricted or locked areas, away from the general collections.

Mark designated staff entrances on your floor plan. If staff areas are not included on the basic floor plan, then create your own plan for each floor of every building. You might want to do this anyway just to keep the information separate from that which is compiled for the public areas of the building. Be certain to share a copy with the disaster response team and have copies available during an emergency for public safety personnel (fire, police, and emergency medical personnel).

EMERGENCY EXITS, LIGHTS, ALARMS, AND SIGNAGE

Take a walk through the staff area of each floor, looking for emergency exits, exit signs, emergency lighting, and signage. Just as you did with the public areas, determine where the emergency exits go. Does the door open onto a stairwell? If so, is it clear which direction takes you out of the building? If the door opens to the outside, are there any obstructions? Place information and a map by the emergency exits leading to the outside that tell staff members where to gather after evacuating the building. Mark the area clearly on a map so new staff members are able to identify the correct location. Indicate which exits are handicapped-accessible.

While checking where emergency exits lead to, confirm that the alarm systems work and that they alert security that someone is leaving the building by that particular door.

Now take a look at the emergency exit signs. Are they visible in the staff areas? Do the signs and their emergency lights activate when there is a power failure? Some of these emergency signs should be connected to a generator. Are there signs at floor level (in case of heavy smoke) directing staff to the emergency exits? If there are no emergency exits in the staff areas, which doors provide the swiftest access to public emergency exits? Post signs to direct staff to these exits.

Check the alarm system to determine if it is audible and visible in the staff areas. Just because it is audible in the public area does not mean that the speaker system or alarm system can be heard or seen anywhere else in the building.

Put flashlights in strategic locations to assist staff in exiting the building, and mark those locations on your map. There should be enough flashlights to help all staff members. This is extremely important for staff areas that are below ground, have no windows, or are in the center of buildings. Set up a schedule to check the charge on the flashlights to make certain they work. Batteries last only a few years, so replace them on a regular schedule.

Once you have had an evacuation drill for the building, be certain to confirm that all staff did the following:

1. Heard or saw the alarms in the staff areas
2. Evacuated the building
3. Left the building by the nearest emergency exit—either staff or public
4. Found the gathering location

OFFICES AND WORKROOMS

After surveying the entrances and emergency exits, mark which offices and workrooms are where on the map or floor plan. Write the department or function for each room on the map. Indicate the locations of any collections in staff areas and note what types of materials they contain. Mark the rooms that have windows. Confirm that the windows opening below ground, at ground level, and onto terraces and stairwells are closed and locked at the end of each working day to prevent access to the building after hours. Check to see if there are alarms to indicate if window glass is broken or windows are open. If your institution does not have "broken glass" alarms, consider having them installed on all windows below the second floor.

Keep an eye out for any potential security and safety issues such as doors to the outside of the building that are propped open or blocked by cabinets. Emergency exit doors should be closed at all times. Any emergency exit doors that are blocked off by furniture or locked with deadbolts should be unblocked or unlocked so they are accessible in case of emergency.

DOORS BETWEEN PUBLIC AREAS AND STAFF AREAS

Look at the entrances from the public to the staff areas of the building. How does one gain access to the staff areas? If the doors open by key or key card/keypad, then confirm that the doors swing shut and automatically relock. Take a look at the offices and workrooms in those areas; are they physically accessible to the public? If so, what types of safety measures are in place to prevent unauthorized entrance? Consider the types of things staff leave in their offices: personal valuables such as purses and wallets, cell phones, and PDAs. There are often computers, laptops, peripherals, and other types of office equipment—not to mention materials from the collection—that have not been checked out and are sitting in offices. Keeping the doors between the public and staff areas locked is important for both the security of your collections and the safety of your staff members.

Perhaps your library or archive cannot afford a security system. Then how does the staff know if anyone enters a nonpublic area? No one wants to be working in a workroom or office and suddenly find an unauthorized individual wandering about in the staff area or, worse, that this unaccompanied person has stolen personal or institutional property.

Set up some type of safety alarm or code to alert the staff in public areas that there is trouble in the nonpublic part of the library. This alarm should sound at the circulation, reference, or security desk. Test the system to see how long it takes to get a response.

STORAGE ROOMS

Using your floor plan, locate the storage areas in each building. Storage areas tend to be in basements, attics, and out-of-the-way areas of libraries and archives. When you survey these areas, you are looking for safety issues for staff members who might be alone in the room(s). Set up a system so that staff members know who is working in the storage area.

Indicate which storage rooms are actively used and which individuals or what departments have access to what storage rooms. Confirm that the doors to these storage areas lock automatically and that there is an emergency exit or a way to get out if someone is accidentally locked inside.

What types of safety precautions are there in these storage areas? Are there emergency lights and signs? Where are the regular light switches? There should be switches both inside and outside the storage rooms. Is there an emergency exit from the rooms, or do people have to go out the main door? Is there more than one entrance to the storage area? Is the storage area sectioned off into cages or rooms? And if so, how do you know if any other staff member is working in one of the storage rooms? (See the checklist "Storage Areas" in appendix A.)

Check to see if there is an emergency alarm or a phone to notify security of problems that arise while working in the storage area. Is there some way that security knows there is a staff member working in the storage area? Set up a protocol to notify security or the department in charge of the storage area when a staff member is going to work there for a period of time, especially after hours.

If someone is in the storage area, can they hear or see emergency and fire alarms? Would they know which way is out if there is no power? Make certain that there is a flashlight by the door and that the emergency lighting works when the power goes off. Indicate clearly the way to the emergency exits from the storage areas.

If the storage areas are below ground, look for signs of insect and water damage. Make certain to notify the preservation department and the facilities and maintenance department if there are any signs of infestation. If the emergency exit from the below-ground storage area opens into a below-ground stairway, does the door open freely, and are the stairs cleared for easy egress? Is there evidence of water seepage from below the door? If so, notify the buildings and grounds department to have the drains cleaned and have the preservation department check for mold and mildew.

MECHANICAL ROOMS

Almost every library or archive building has some type of mechanical room even if the building is on a large campus. Mechanical rooms contain some or all of the following equipment: boilers, furnaces, HVAC systems, water heaters, sprinkler system shutoff valves, electrical boxes, and shutoff valves for water, electrical, and gas. In some instances libraries may have more than one mechanical room, especially if the rare books/special collections and the computer services/information technology (IT) departments have their own HVAC systems.

These mechanical rooms should be locked at all times, except when facilities and maintenance staff members are servicing the equipment. No contractor should be in the mechanical room without supervision by the facilities and maintenance department staff.

Each mechanical room should have its own alarm system indicating fire, malfunctioning equipment, and standing water. Make certain the fire and smoke alarms are working properly and that security or the facilities and maintenance department knows which alarms indicate what problems. Alarms should sound when sump pumps activate, indicating the equipment is functioning because of excess water. Water alarms should ring to indicate standing water. The facilities and maintenance department should be notified so they can fix the problem. Although the aforementioned items are usually included in a disaster response plan, mechanical equipment failure can damage collections and be a security concern for the well-being of staff members.

Check to see if there are sprinklers or some other type of fire suppression system in the mechanical room. In addition, this may be the room where the water shutoff valve for the sprinkler system is located. If so, does the facilities and maintenance department know how to turn off the water and the sprinkler system? Is the valve secured against tampering?

All valves and shutoffs should be marked to indicate what turns off what. If special equipment or instructions are necessary to disable or turn off valves, place that information nearby so facilities and maintenance personnel or the fire department can turn them off.

Check to see that the emergency lighting is working in the mechanical rooms. Confirm that emergency evacuation alarms are audible and visible in the mechanical rooms and that exits are clearly marked and illuminated. If the mechanical room contains an emergency exit leading out of the building, is it accessible, and does an alarm ring if the door is opened?

Someone on the building's staff should know which mechanical rooms control what areas and whom to contact if alarms are heard within. This is especially important for mechanical rooms that service special collections, rare book rooms, and computer systems/IT departments. Each of these departments has different environmental standards for its collections or equipment. Loss of a controlled environment will adversely affect the department's ability to function properly.

Establish a good working relationship with the facilities and maintenance department staff who service the mechanical rooms in your building. Learn what they can and cannot do to help control the environment in the building and what types of safety devices are built into the room and the equipment.

STAFF LOUNGES, KITCHENS, AND RESTROOMS

These rooms are often located outside the normal staff traffic pattern. They are also rooms where staff members congregate for socializing before and after hours, so staff may not pay attention to alarms and evacuation drills. Be certain to check the kitchens, lounges, and restrooms to confirm the building is empty during an emergency.

Take a good look at these rooms to see if there are fire alarms located inside or nearby. Can you hear or see the alarms go off from inside the lounge, kitchen, and restrooms? Are there emergency exit signs above the doors? Does your staff know how to exit the building from these rooms?

Check to see if there is emergency lighting in the kitchen, lounge, and restrooms. Test the emergency lights to confirm they function during a power outage. Keep flashlights in a logical place and make certain all staff members know where they are.

If the kitchen is connected to a public meeting room, is there a way to close off that facility from the meeting room? This will prevent the public from entering the library or archive when the building is closed to the public. It will also prevent the public from entering staff areas without authorization.

MEETING ROOMS IN STAFF AREAS

When surveying the staff areas, take a look at the meeting and conference rooms that are set aside for internal use. Indicate on your floor plan where they are located within the building, and mark their entrances and exits. Look for alarms, emergency lighting, and emergency exit signs. Check to make certain the emergency lighting works when the power is off. Confirm that the alarms are audible and visible in the meeting rooms.

Are the staff meeting and seminar rooms available for meetings of professionals who are not members of the staff? Does the library or archive hold professional workshops, meetings, or seminars in these staff meeting rooms? Establish a procedure so that a staff member or security guard is required to bring participants to the room. At the end of the session, staff members should escort the participants out of the staff area.

If your staff members wear ID badges when in the building, then any member of the public coming into the staff areas must have a visitor's badge. Security staff should keep track of the badges and make certain they are returned when the meeting or seminar is over. All badges should be accounted for at the end of the day.

Part

2

SECURITY FOR COLLECTIONS AND EQUIPMENT

Chapter 4

Security for General Collections

Library collections are expensive to acquire, process, and house. They can be difficult, if not impossible, to replace if stolen or damaged. Even if your library focuses its collecting policy on popular reading and reference materials, the cost of replacing these materials when they have been stolen or damaged can become prohibitive. In these days of budget cuts and minimal spending, libraries should be able to use scarce resources not to replace items, but to build new and heavily used collections.

To this end, establish policies that hold patrons accountable for deliberate damage to collections, including (but not restricted to) the common problems of slitting out pages, pictures, and journal or encyclopedia articles; removing text blocks from covers; and stealing audiovisual and digital materials. These policies should be enforced by suspension of library privileges and by arrest for multiple and serious infractions.

PROTECTING CIRCULATING RESOURCES

Some libraries have sought to reduce the amount of damage and destruction—specifically, slitting out pages—done to their print materials by reducing the cost of photocopying to five or ten cents per page and by offering ledger-size paper for copying two pages at a time. Others have extended their circulation periods to four weeks with additional renewal periods, allowing people to have the items in their possession until they are done reading a book or viewing a video. Renewal from home, online or by telephone, also alleviates the hassle for patrons of bringing books back to renew them. Nevertheless, there are still those patrons who take books from their covers or just don't bother to return books, and still others who don't bother to check books out in the first place.

Having security guards check all outgoing patrons and staff for library materials to confirm that those materials are checked out is essential. Having security gates that detect electronic or magnetic targets inserted in the books is highly effective. Unfortunately, many small library systems cannot afford the price of these security measures. In such cases, at the very minimum, circulation-desk staff members need to be near the exit so that staff can watch who is leaving with what in their hands and bags. If the library has a self-checkout system for materials and no security guards or devices, then staff members must be extra vigilant of the habits and actions of patrons when they leave the building.

Tattle-Tape security strips and targets have been around for many years now. The former is inserted into the spine of a hardcover book or between pages in a paperback; the latter under the flyleaf or on the back cover of a book. These security devices ring when a person walks through security gates with a book. Some libraries deactivate the devices when the item is checked out and reactivate them upon their return. There are even some libraries that use these security devices but don't have a security system. Bookstores, drugstores, and electronics stores use similar devices to prevent theft. (For a list of the various options available for protecting collection materials, see "General Collections: Security of the Collection" in appendix A.)

The newest inventory security technology used in libraries is radio frequency identification (RFID). This technology lets you send, store, and retrieve data remotely.[1] RFID is a tiny radio transmitter that can be programmed with all types of information. The device can be as small as a microdot or as large as a traditional security strip.

RFID was first used by commercial businesses to keep a constant inventory of their products, from the warehouse to the consumer.[2] RFID is now widely available for use in securing public collections in libraries and archives. An RFID target, called a tag, inserted into books and audiovisual cases may solve some of the problems of tracking and checking out these materials. The cost averages about one dollar per device with installation, hardware, and software. According to Dennis Chaptman, the devices themselves are ten to twelve cents each.[3] Libraries are starting to put these devices into their collections, and museums are using the devices to mark and identify high-theft items in their collections. The use of RFID in libraries will likely become more widespread as the price becomes more affordable and the technology to track the materials is customized for library and archive purposes.

RFID circulation systems make it possible to check out materials to a specific patron automatically as the materials are taken out the door, and check the items back in when they are returned. Of course, there are some security issues that revolve around privacy for our patrons. The American Library Association (ALA) has published guidelines for RFID use in libraries as it pertains to intellectual freedom.[4]

Most libraries put security strips or targets of some type into books and, in academic libraries, inside journals. Some public libraries put security strips inside magazines that have a long retention schedule. But what about the nonprint items in our collections? Protecting them requires more vigilance and ingenuity. Some libraries tried putting magnetic strips on the label side of CDs. This caused real problems because the discs became unbalanced, or the adhesive released, causing the discs to stick inside players, damaging them irreparably. So libraries discontinued that practice. There are security devices that can be placed around the hub or hole of a CD or DVD. These devices are effective as long as the adhesive remains stable. Once the adhesive releases, the target can shift, destabilizing the disc so it doesn't play properly.

With the introduction of any new format or medium, there are increased instances of theft and damage. When videos were first introduced in libraries, the cassettes quickly walked out the door, particularly the most popular titles. Many libraries kept the cassettes behind circulation desks, thereby requiring the staff to find each item. This decreased the amount of outright theft, but increased demands on staff time. The same was true of CDs in music collections.

Today DVDs seem to be the item of choice for theft and damage. In the first two years that DVDs were introduced to libraries, more than 50 percent of them were checked out and never returned. Some never even circulated, disappearing from technical services or shelving departments. Others were checked out once and were never seen again. Libraries must purchase and circulate the newest audiovisual format once it is prevalent in patrons' homes. In addition to being high-theft items, DVDs and CDs are physically more fragile than video- and audiocassette tapes, especially when put into book drops. A good number are damaged by the users and by the hub lock in the disc cases. Nevertheless, it is the high rate of disappearance that is most distressing, and it is difficult to forestall deliberate theft.

CDs, videos, and DVDs are particularly susceptible to theft. It is easy to remove the items from their protective enclosures and take the disc or cassette, leaving the case on the shelf. In addition, patrons may take the whole item out of the library and then just return the case empty or with something other than the matching recording inside it. In this case, it is imperative that circulation staff look at the title on the case and on the disc or cassette to be certain they are the same.

The loss or theft of collections should result in blocking patrons' library cards, fining them for the cost of replacing the item, or filing charges with local authorities for recovery of the items and restitution for the theft. Of course, because of the character and nature of libraries, we give patrons the benefit of the doubt. It is important to track the amnesty granted to patrons. If and when a patron abuses this goodwill, then the library administrators must charge the patron with theft. It is important that the library administration encourage the police to pursue and prosecute the theft and enforce the policy prohibiting theft of collections. Without follow-through, these policies prohibiting damage and theft are unenforceable and just lead to more theft. Pamela Cravey's book *Protecting Library Staff, Users, Collections, and Facilities* contains a detailed discussion differentiating loss from theft.[5]

Libraries institute a variety of safeguards to prevent the theft of items by patrons with library cards. Almost all require potential patrons to show proof of address such as a driver's license or utility bill. Other libraries mail a card to new patrons, and upon its receipt the patrons receive a card and can check out materials. Still other libraries limit the number of items that can be checked out the first few times the card is used. This allows the library time to confirm addresses and make certain that materials are returned on time. There is always a way around these safeguards. It is the few who take advantage of the laxness and loopholes within these procedures who force the restrictions on the majority of honest patrons.

PROTECTING NONCIRCULATING MATERIALS IN GENERAL COLLECTIONS

Noncirculating materials in a general collection include reference materials, microforms, photographs, and vertical file materials. These collections are usually more expensive to acquire and usually cannot be replaced. They provide in-depth information or basic background information on a variety of topics.

Noncirculating reference materials include encyclopedias and specialized dictionaries, indexes, and almanacs. They are expensive to purchase and may be impossible to replace, especially if one volume of a set is damaged or stolen. To prevent loss, they should be marked with the library's identifying marks, and also with security devices. Noncirculating reference materials that show up at the circulation desk should be held and returned to the correct department as soon as possible. Circulation and reference staff might try to locate a circulating copy of a reference title for a patron, since in public libraries especially, there may be circulating copies in other locations within the system. Placing photocopiers near these noncirculating collections makes it easier for users to copy whatever they desire.

Microforms (microfilm and microfiche) almost never circulate in public libraries. By locating microform readers and reader-printers within the collections, and by keeping the copying costs to a minimum, libraries can encourage patrons to use these invaluable materials. Library staff members need to clean the microfilm readers and reader-printers regularly and have them serviced often to prevent damage to these expensive collections. The newest microfilm reader-printers scan the images to computers for easy downloading and e-mailing to patrons.

Some libraries will not allow users to retrieve or, more particularly, to refile microfiche. This is because the sheets of film are easy to misfile. Once the fiche is misfiled, it may never be located again. Replacing a single sheet of microfiche may be impossible, and the cost of replacing the entire series may be prohibitive. As for rolls of microfilm, they are easy enough to put back into boxes and drawers. As long as the correct roll is in its proper box, there should be minimal misshelving. Almost all microfilm created as part of an archival project has an eye-legible title or target at the beginning of the roll. So if you find a number of microfilm rolls without boxes, you can tell which roll goes in which box. Microfilm that is 16 mm or that is not made for libraries and archives may not have eye-legible titles. It is especially important to teach users to place rolls of film in their appropriate boxes after use so the rolls do not get lost or misplaced.

Photographs do not tend to circulate unless they are part of an art collection or an educational program, so refiling photographs in the correct folders and drawers is crucial to prevent "loss." In many cases, photographs are part of special collections and archives, so their use and reshelving are controlled by the staff.

Vertical files containing clippings, pamphlets, and other small items are difficult if not impossible to control. Some libraries circulate the contents of these collections, while others hold them as strictly noncirculating items. Still other institutions permit users to take out parts of vertical files. Of those that circulate, some of the materials are cataloged and some have specific circulation periods. Over the years, vertical files may weed themselves as the most popular items disappear. In most cases, unless the vertical file is part of the noncirculating reference collection, there is probably no way to control loss to this part of the collection.

In the case of genealogy and local history collections, as well as special collections or archives, those vertical file materials tend to be reference items that can be copied upon request. Again, it may be difficult to control random loss. Larger items should be cataloged, stapled, or sewn into pamphlets and shelved within the collection.

Three-dimensional objects such as games, toys, and artwork may circulate as part of the library's collection. Libraries tend to assign these objects limited circulation periods. Circulation staff members must confirm that all parts are returned at the end of the circulation period and that patrons are fined for losses.

MOVING MATERIALS TO SPECIAL OR NONCIRCULATING COLLECTIONS

Librarians sometimes come across materials that are older, rare, or valuable while weeding or reviewing collections. In some cases the materials are fragile or brittle and require special storage conditions, handling, and treatment. If your institution has a special collections or rare book room, move these materials to that part of the building. The Association of College and Research Libraries (ACRL) has a policy that describes how to complete this type of intra-institutional transfer.[6] Transferring older materials to special collections protects the items from additional physical damage and minimizes theft, because special collections restrict users and their actions. Some libraries routinely transfer materials that were published prior to 1850, or in some cases 1900, to special collections to protect them. The same policy may be applied to holdings in a specific subject area. Not all old items are rare or valuable or even vulnerable. These items may remain in circulating collections until they are worn out and discarded.

Alternatively, older materials in need of protection can be placed into the reference or noncirculating general collection. This might be done if the main branch of a library system retains "last copies" or if the item is in better condition than the one in reference. If a library system has a "last copy" in circulation and the reference copy is in worse shape than this circulating copy, the librarian may decide to discard the reference copy and put the circulating copy in its place. Although this option protects the older materials from future circulation, it does not necessarily protect them from theft. If you think they are high-theft items, then consider moving them to special collections as described above.

PROTECTING COLLECTIONS IN STAFF AREAS

One of the great perks of working in a library or archive is that you get to see all the new materials as they arrive. This is an even bigger perk in acquisitions, technical services, and collections maintenance—the departments where materials are first accessioned and processed. The items come in and you get to look at them, handle them, and put them on your desk for further perusal. That's a great perk, except when the books don't get accessioned and processed, and therefore don't make it to the shelf for a while. On rare occasions, they don't make it to the shelf, ever. Obviously, this should never happen. Staff members should check out materials even if they sit on their desks. This is a good way to prevent "lost" items.

Every library, archive, historical society, and museum has unprocessed materials in its technical services or storage areas. These items were purchased, acquired, or donated but have not yet been accessioned, cataloged, or processed. Take a look at the location in your institution where these items are stored.

In institutions with circulating collections, determine who has access to these materials before they are processed and cataloged. Are materials shelved or stacked next to the loading dock or delivery entrance after they are received? How long do these new items wait until they are processed, cataloged, added to the circulation system, and placed on the shelves? Knowing the answers to these questions can alert you to a potentially risky stage of your processing system. Place newly received items away from loading dock doors, delivery entrances, and doors near public areas. Implement some type of check-in system to confirm that all items that arrive are processed and sent out for shelving. Ultimately, this will decrease internal theft.

The same is true for materials for the reference collection. They should be accessioned, processed, and cataloged so they can be located within the reference parts of the collection. Indeed, this holds true for collections in institutions where materials never circulate, that is, archives, rare books and special collections, historical societies, and museums. Materials should be accessioned so that a user can at least identify that a collection exists and can determine where it is located.[7]

Where do you store noncirculating materials prior to accessioning and cataloging? Discuss procedures for receipt of these items with the special collections, rare books, or archives department staff. Create a procedure to move these items out of the circulating materials' receiving or technical services area and into secured storage as soon as possible. In most institutions, newly acquired noncirculating materials are delivered and housed in the archives and special collections department. After the items have been accessioned, they can sit for years awaiting processing, during which time they are usually inaccessible and unavailable to the public. If this is the case, how does the staff ensure the materials do not leave the area without a way to track them?

Nonprocessed collections and items should rarely be given to a patron. Some basic record should exist before the material is used. This is especially true of rare and valuable materials housed in special collections, rare book rooms, and archives. (See also chapter 5, "Security for Special Collections and Archives.")

Cataloged materials can end up on a staff member's desk or in her office while she is doing research or working on a special project. As staff members, we have a tendency to take materials to our desks without checking them out, especially if we think it will be for a very short while. The next thing you know, the book has been there for months and the catalog is now showing the title as missing. The library should establish a policy for staff members and books in offices. These titles should be checked out just the same way that books leaving the building or books going to the bindery are checked out. If the book is going to be on display, it also needs to be checked out to that location. Checking out materials is particularly important if staff members take reference and noncirculating items to their offices for a research project. The location code on those books should also be changed to reflect that office. Create a series of locations for internal use and use them for internal circulation. You can even use these special circulation locations when keeping statistics for noncirculating collections.

No matter what the routine is for delivery and accession of materials into your collection, you need to create a procedure that tracks the items from the time they enter the building until they are processed for shelving and retrieval by staff members and the public.

Establish a fixed routine so that technical services staff accession, process, catalog, and add items to the circulation and cataloging system before these items leave the area. You might even set up a routine for "rushing" the high-demand items through processing so that reserves can be filled right away. For those libraries that receive their books already processed, be certain to check that the materials are in the circulation system before allowing staff members to take them away from the department. Again, circulating materials should be checked out even if they are going to be used in-house. In cases of long-term, in-house use, create a location for such items. For example, if a department purchases a title as part of its professional collection, there should be a location code for that department. If a book arrived in damaged condition and is sent to the bindery or collections maintenance department, it should be given the appropriate location code until it is in usable condition. In this way, materials are accounted for and items do not "disappear" into the bowels of the library.

Notes

1. Molly Wood, "RFID: Bring It On," C/Net, *The Buzz Report* (February 2005), http://www.cnet.com/4520-6033_1-6223038-1.html. Another story warns about potential flaws: Robert Vamos, "Psst. Your Shiny New Passport Has a Computer Virus," C/Net, *Security Watch* (March 17, 2006), http://reviews.cnet.com/4520-3513_7-6466679-1.html.
2. Dennis Chaptman, "Tag—You're IDed: UW Research Is Helping Share the Radio-Frequency Revolution," *On Wisconsin* 107, no. 1 (Spring 2006): 14.
3. Ibid.
4. American Library Association, "RFID in Libraries: Privacy and Confidentiality Guidelines," 2006, http://www.ala.org/ala/oif/statementspols/otherpolicies/rfidguidelines.cfm.
5. Cravey, *Protecting Library Staff,* 29–32.
6. Association of College and Research Libraries, "Guidelines on the Selection of General Collection Materials for Transfer to Special Collections," 2nd ed. 1994, rev. 1999, http://www.ala.org/ala/acrl/acrlstandards/guidelinesselection.cfm.
7. There is a long discussion about the basic processing of archival collections in Mark A. Greene and Dennis Meissner, "More Product, Less Process: Revamping Traditional Archival Processing," *American Archivist* 68, no. 2 (Fall/Winter 2005): 208–63.

Chapter 5

Security for Special Collections and Archives

CASE STUDY

As a standing policy and procedure, the archives and special collections reading room of a certain library was constantly monitored by a staff member at the reference desk while patrons accessed folders and boxes of special collections and archives materials at reading tables. The floors holding the special collections and archives materials were locked to prevent access when the reading room was not open. The stacks were all closed to the public, accessible only by the department's staff.

Included in the holdings was a rare pamphlet collection. Despite the department's precautions and unbeknownst to the curators and librarians, the collection was stolen. One day, perhaps years after the initial theft, a researcher requested the pamphlet collection and discovered that the contents of the envelopes were not what was described on the envelopes. It was assumed that bit by bit, the pamphlets had been taken out of their archival folders and sleeves and replaced with used items of no value. Because the collection was housed in envelopes that were not see-through, there was no way to detect the substitution at the time of the theft. In all, thousands of dollars' worth of the collection was stolen.

The curators, archivists, and librarians felt it was a member of the staff who had taken those items, but many patrons had viewed the collection over the years. The police never found the items or identified the thief. They suggested additional procedures to prevent future theft of the special collections and archives materials, including lockers located outside the collections areas for all staff and student workers, additional cameras, and tighter inventory control of requested items. They suggested that the staff look at the requested materials before returning them to the closed stacks. Of course, if a staff member steals from the collections, then it might still be many years before the theft is realized.

This scenario illustrates the importance of comprehensive security processes for special collections that may well exceed the norm. Special collections departments should keep careful records detailing the history of use of their collections. This helps pinpoint previous use of the materials and perhaps the identity of a thief. Maintaining a history of the users of specific items in a library or archive is contrary to the standard policy of anonymity that many institutions adhere to. Most circulation systems delete user information immediately after each item is returned. However, for special collections and archives, this consideration for patron privacy must be weighed against the risk that such anonymity poses to the security of rare or valuable collections.[1] (See the checklist "Patron Using Collections" in appendix A.)

SURVEYING THE SPECIAL COLLECTIONS AND ARCHIVES

Begin your survey of the special collections and archives in the same manner as all the other collections and buildings. Work from the outside in, examining entrances and access to the reading rooms, offices, storage rooms, and stacks areas. (See the checklist "Protecting Special Collections, Rare Books, and Archives" in appendix A.)

If the special collections or archives department is on the ground floor or on a floor with walkout access to the outside, survey the outside of the building first to note where the emergency exits are, where the windows are, and how accessible they are. There should be alarms on the windows at ground level or below ground level. These alarms should be wired to indicate if the windows are open or if the glass is broken.

When the special collections or archives are in a separate building, there should be only one entrance to be used by staff and patrons alike. Look at the loading dock or delivery entrance. The doors should be locked at all times except when a delivery is in progress. The deliveries should be monitored by security or staff. The doors should be locked with key cards or keypad locks, with a very limited number of people having codes. Movement outside or inside these doors should activate security cameras that should record all activity. The taping system should not overwrite the tapes. Security tapes should be kept for at least thirty days, if not longer. Put external lights on motion detectors.

After completing a survey of the outside of the building, begin a survey of the area where the special collections and archives are located. (See the checklist "Department Survey: Special Collections" in appendix A.) Walk around the floor and note the doors that provide access to the reading room and the stacks area. There should only be one door into the reading room. The doors into the stacks area should be locked and accessible only by special collections or archives staff members. If there is an elevator or stairway in the area, does it open into the special collections area? Is special collections and archives the only department on that floor? If so, then arrange to lock off the floor when it is closed to the public and when there are no staff members present. Do the same with the stairwell, as long as this is not a violation of fire codes for your state.

If there is a door between the reading room and the storage or closed stacks area, determine how traffic is controlled between the two areas. The door should be locked when the reading room is not open. The staff member in the reading room should monitor all people who enter and exit through that door. No member of the public should be permitted in the closed stacks or storage area without supervision.

In addition, all emergency exit doors should have alarms that ring both in the area and in the security department or at the local police department. Windows and skylights should be locked and be part of the alarm system. If there are windows on the ground level that open, they should have bars or gates that prevent unauthorized access, especially when they open into storage or closed stacks areas.

Motion detectors should monitor closed stacks and storage areas at all times, and reading rooms after hours to prevent unauthorized access. The motion detectors should sound an alarm at the security desk or the local police station. When used in conjunction with security cameras, motion detectors will help security guards pinpoint the intruder.

All alarms and security devices should be hardwired into the institution's electrical system and be included in the systems powered by emergency backup generators when there is no power.

SECURITY

Staff access to all the nonpublic areas of rare books, special collections, and archives should be controlled through the use of keys, key cards, or keypads. If you purchase a key card system, it should be able to limit and track access to specific rooms and areas and should keep a detailed log of the date, time, and location the key card was used and by whom.

Key cards to the special collections and archives should be set to limit access to secure areas. For instance, if you have a temporary worker, volunteer, or student worker who needs access to the workrooms for office equipment or basic supplies, their keycard should limit their access to just those areas. If senior staff require access to storage and highly secured areas, their key cards should permit this. Security should be able to monitor the movements of people via their key cards to determine if they are in unauthorized areas and when. No persons should be given key cards that provide access to secured areas without the authorization of the head of archives and special collections. Non-employees should not be permitted in staff areas without supervision by a staff member. If non-employees, such as contractors and consultants, are given access to storage areas for special projects, their temporary key cards should permit access only to those specific areas. Their movements should be monitored closely. At no time should non-employees be permitted to remove items from storage areas without supervision by the head of archives and special collections or by the person responsible for hiring the contractor or consultant.

If there is a bell for patrons to use for access to the rare books, special collections, or archives, set it to ring in both the reading room and the closed stacks area. This way, if the reading room is empty, staff will know there is a user seeking entry.

LOCKERS

Most if not all special collections, rare book rooms, and archives have lockers located just outside the entrance for patrons to leave their coats and other belongings. These lockers should be secure and close with a key. Some lockers are designed to return coins, while others merely use a key. Either kind is suitable for archives and special collections. All researchers must place their personal belongings, papers, bags, pens, and other objects into the lockers. If there are no lockers, then a separate area should be designated for the storage of all personal objects while researchers are using the reading room. Post a list online and beside the lockers itemizing what is permitted in the special collections and archives reading room.

USER REGISTRATION

User registration protects the collection from theft, provides user statistics, and allows staff to track which users are requesting what items. Most institutions require picture identification, and some (including the National Archives and the Library of Congress) require a reader to obtain a photo ID that is renewed on a regular basis.[2] If a researcher is visiting regularly and doing long-term research, you might not require that person to register each time he enters the special collections room. Some institutions will require registration each time; others will issue a card to the user that has a short expiration date. A user registration form should collect information about the researcher's intended use of the materials consulted. (See the "Special Collections Department Patron Registration Form" in appendix B.) The form should reiterate the use and access policies of the special collections or archives unit.

A separate procedures or use policy statement should be given to each researcher when he enters the special collections. You might also put an abbreviated list of restrictions and use policies on each research desk. (Two examples of use policies for special collections can be found in appendix B.)

RESTRICTIONS

Restricting what patrons can bring into special collections, rare book rooms, and archives is standard policy.[3] Post the restrictions and a list of permitted items in the locker area and give the list to all researchers when they enter the building. Post the permitted items on your website so researchers can decide what to bring with them. Today, most institutions permit laptops and PDAs in their reading rooms. Some institutions permit scanners and digital cameras, although others do not. All electronic equipment should be registered by staff or security and accounted for when that person exits the building. Some institutions may make electronic devices available for users upon request. Use and security policies range from permitting researchers to bring in their own writing materials (pencils and paper), notes, and files to restricting materials to blank paper (often some color, changed on some irregular basis) and pencils only. Either security or the reference staff should look at all materials as patrons leave the reading room and the building. Security should confirm that all electronic devices in the researcher's possession are the ones brought in. At the end of the day, check to see that personal belongings were removed from all the lockers. Any remaining materials should be held by the security staff for retrieval by the patron.

THE READING ROOM

The reading room or reference area should be laid out so that the working surfaces of the tables are visible from the reference desk. If there are hidden areas, these should be visible to security cameras placed to show what is happening on the surface of the table. The person at the reference desk must then monitor both the cameras and the tables themselves.

Chairs should be placed at the tables so that the patrons all face the same direction. Some institutions have the users face the reference desk, while others have users face away from it. Direct line of sight from the reference desk to the patron is best in order to prevent anyone from surreptitiously removing or mutilating collections.

If the special collections and archives policy permits laptops, scanners, and digital cameras, then the reference staff must be diligent in reviewing the fragility of materials prior to giving them to patrons. This will decrease the risk of possible damage by patrons when they handle or scan items. An automatic or sheet-fed scanner should never be used for flat materials in archival and special collections. The rules for appropriate use of electronic devices, proper handling of collections, and staff supervision of such activities should be clearly stated in writing and prominently displayed on reading room tables. In some archives and special collections, only the staff are allowed to photograph or scan their collections.

USE OF COLLECTIONS

Reference room staff should be alert in watching patrons' actions and should circulate around the room on an irregular basis to see that all is in order. Reference staff should make a visual inspection of the tables, especially when patrons are using folders from a large collection of manuscript or printed materials.

Take a look at the materials before handing them to the researcher. What is in the file? What do the materials look like? What is their physical condition? When the file is returned, look again. If the researcher requests a box of files, give them one file at a time. Upon completing research for that period of time or that day, examine the researchers' folders and papers to confirm that they did not accidentally take any manuscript or photographic materials. (See the checklist "Special Collections: Use of the Collection" in appendix A.)

Research staff should be careful not to become lax around regular researchers, especially those who are librarians and archivists. There are articles in the professional literature and in the news about professors, librarians, and archivists stealing or mutilating rare collections.[4] Staff should continuously monitor activity in the reading rooms, never permit researchers into the stacks and storage areas, and never leave the reading room unattended. Schedules should be set so that there is always a backup staff member available to cover the reading room.

IDENTIFYING OR MARKING THE COLLECTION

There are those in the rare book and special collections field who advocate never marking collections with property stamps because it decreases their monetary value and changes the actual items. However, if there is no way to identify the items in the special collections, archives, and rare books collections that belong to your institution, then it may be impossible for you to prove an item is part of your collection should it be stolen or removed without permission. In addition, you could find that your valuable items have not only been stolen but have been sold through the rare book market to private collections, never to be seen again.

In earlier times, libraries and archives routinely stamped, marked, labeled, and processed every item purchased by or donated to the institution. This process included stamping the fore-edge, the title page, and the "secret" page with the library's name; labeling the spine; placing book pockets in the book; and bar-coding the item. Many rare book and special collections were created from volumes in general circulation that are now rare, unusual, have an early imprint date, or have some other special characteristic, such as embossed or illustrated covers. Do not remove the old markings and labels from these materials before housing them in special collections.

New items added to special and rare book collections today are labeled or marked using nondamaging materials. These items are not usually stamped with library property stamps, but have small, discrete labels printed on acid-free, pH-neutral paper and are affixed using a polyvinyl acrylic (PVA) adhesive that has permanent adhesion properties but will not yellow, become brittle, or release over time. PVA does not introduce damaging chemicals into the paper, and it will not leave acidic stains.

As part of the accession of materials into rare book and special collections, each volume or item has an accession number. This is a unique identification number, much like a bar code, that connects the item to an acquisitions folder or provenance file. The accession number, or in the case of archives, collection identification number (or records group number), should be written in a uniform place within the volume or on the back of the loose item using a soft lead pencil.

This basic processing procedure of affixing a property label or mark and adding an accession number should be performed when the item arrives at the repository.[5] No archival items without a preliminary inventory or collection-level finding aid should circulate or be loaned or used by researchers.[6] A request for an unprocessed or minimally processed item is often the rationale for selecting the next items for a more thorough processing.[7]

Fragile items should be duplicated using a photocopier or a scanner. Use these duplicates for public access and research. Place a property mark or stamp on each photocopied duplicate, along with some notation that indicates its status as a duplicate and its collection number.

Digital copies, especially those available online, should have digital watermarks embedded into the image and the coding.[8] The digital watermark should contain the name of the institution, the date of creation, and some type of information that connects it to the collection. Digital copies should be low-resolution images in order to discourage theft and publication without authorization or permission of the copyright holder.[9]

TRUE SECURITY RISKS WITHIN COLLECTIONS

Not everything in a rare book room, special collection, or archive is rare or valuable. Some materials are there because of their age, some for their unusual bindings or paper, and others because they are less common. In the case of archives, many items are unique, containing one-of-a-kind letters, memoranda, and photographs. All these special collections run the added risk that they have been segregated from the general circulating collection and are perceived as valuable. So what are the "true" security risks? Items that have a monetary value, have some type of artistic significance, or provoke a "strong emotional or acquisitive reaction" are most at risk of theft.[10] If at all possible, especially in the case of archives, these types of items should be duplicated or digitized and the originals stored in a safe, secure location. The duplicates or surrogates should be given to the researcher to use.

Items in special collections, rare book rooms, and archives are valuable or at risk because they are wanted by others. Some people are true collectors looking for objects that complete their collections, while others are just seeking the unusual. They want to own these materials, regardless of the damage their removal causes to the original object.[11] Items at risk for this type of theft include maps, photographic or illustrative plates, drawings, and signatures of famous people.[12]

ASSIGNING RISK OR VALUE TO SPECIAL COLLECTIONS

We need to be cognizant of the value of our rare books and special collections, both in terms of their uniqueness and their monetary worth. This means keeping track of thefts from other institutions, monitoring print and photographic items that come up for sale in auction houses, watching offerings on eBay, and being aware of acquisitions and sales by book dealers.[13] For instance, if there is a bookseller who suddenly has many rare and unusual maps or plates that were originally part of bound volumes, you might survey your collections to see if any of your bound maps are missing, especially if you learn that other libraries and archives are missing theirs.[14]

Of course, the same may be true of items in the general circulating collection and the reference collection; there may be volumes or plates of monetary value within these books. The volumes may have been in the general collection for years and managed to remain intact and usable. These items should be moved into the special collections area and marked appropriately to protect the valuable parts.

STORAGE AREAS FOR SPECIAL COLLECTIONS

If the storage area for a special collection is in active use (as opposed to low use or no use), then at the very least, check that the doors are locked at the end of the working day. If the storage area is seldom used, then confirm who has access to the area and under what circumstances.

STAFF AREAS FOR SPECIAL COLLECTIONS

Look at the route between the reading room and the staff and storage areas. Keep this path free of obstructions and unprocessed collections. This is for the physical safety of the collections as well as the staff. If a collection or item is being used by a researcher for more than one day, then you might keep the items in the staff area overnight. Otherwise, all the materials that are used during the day should be reshelved at the end of the working day to prevent loss after hours.

All collections should be shelved in their proper storage containers when not in use. When staff begin to process or work with unprocessed or partially processed collections, the materials should be worked on in designated areas in the staff room or workroom. At the end of the day, all the items that are being processed should be stored away securely to prevent loss or inadvertent destruction.

Materials that are designated for destruction because they are duplicates or not part of the collection should be segregated from the remaining collection and clearly labeled. Those items that are designated for withdrawal from the collection and are destined for exchange or sale should also be segregated and clearly labeled. Items marked for withdrawal and destruction should be housed in an area separate and distinct from the main collection. Shred sensitive items in-house or through a reputable shredding company, perhaps the same one used by the records management department when records are sent out for destruction.

The staff areas and storage areas for rare books, special collections, and archives should be limited to staff members only. As stated earlier, non-employees working in nonpublic areas should be supervised. Lock all doors between these special collections areas and the rest of the building to prevent unauthorized access. The doors should be locked using key cards or keypads.

SAFE EVACUATION OF COLLECTIONS

Should there be a disaster, where the aftermath is physical damage to buildings so that entry to them cannot be controlled, extra care should be taken to secure rare books, special collections, and archives housed in storage and work areas. You have two basic choices after a disaster: either move the collections to a secure storage area away from the damaged part of the building or to a remote location, or have security guards patrol the area to prevent unauthorized access and loss of materials. The first sounds easier to accomplish, but if the collections are extensive, this may not be feasible. If the special collections and archives department is water-damaged, then focus on stabilizing the physical condition of the collections and the environment of the area. Your disaster response plan should require the special collections areas to be secured and rehabilitated first in the aftermath of a disaster. Secure the windows and doors with boards until they can be replaced. Stabilize the environment as quickly as possible and restrict all access to the department.

If you choose to relocate the special collections or archives to a remote location, select a storage facility that has a stabilized, controlled environment; sufficient space to store the collection in all its boxes; and restricted access. Consider using local records-storage companies for this short-term storage. They usually have a twenty-four-hour emergency phone number, boxes, and an arrangement with a trucking company.

Your choice for securing the contents of rare book, special, and archival collections depends on the scope of the disaster, the type of damage, and the number of staff members available. Discuss the criteria for securing special collections and archives on-site or removing them to remote storage with the disaster response team.[15]

Notes

1. Kim Martineau, "Rare Documents Going Digital: Yale May Join Libraries Using Technology against Theft of Originals," *Hartford Courant,* January 15, 2006, available at http://msn-list.te.verweg.com/2006-January/004165.html; and Alison Leigh Cowan, "Theft Case Rattles Sedate World of Rare Maps," *New York Times,* Arts section, October 3, 2005.
2. Almost every special collection and rare book library has restrictions and guidelines for use of its collections by researchers. One example is the Grolier Club Library. For its guidelines, see http://www.grolierclub.org/library_guidelines_for_res.htm. A standard use policy can be found at http://www.nypl.org/access2/ on the New York Public Library's website.
3. Wesleyan University Special Collections and Archives, "Guidelines for Using Materials in Special Collections and Archives," http://www.wesleyan.edu/libr/schome/general/guidelines.html; and Ohio Historical Society, http://www.ohiohistory.org/resource/archlib/use.html.
4. Greene and Meissner, "More Product, Less Process," 252.
5. Mary Lynn Ritzenthaler, *Preserving Archives and Manuscripts* (Chicago: Society of American Archivists, 1994), 107.
6. Ibid., 108.
7. Greene and Meissner, "More Product, Less Process," 251, 253.
8. Fred Mintzer, Jeffrey Lotspiech, and Norishige Morimoto, "Safeguarding Digital Library Contents and Users: Digital Watermarking," *D-Lib Magazine,* December 1997, http://www.dlib.org/dlib/december97/ibm/12lotspiech.html.
9. There are some excellent works on copyright and intellectual property available, including Carrie Russell, *Complete Copyright: An Everyday Guide for Librarians* (Chicago: American Library Association, 2004); and Kenneth D. Crews, *Copyright Law for Librarians and Educators: Creative Strategies and Practical Solutions,* 2nd ed. (Chicago: American Library Association, 2005). You can also consult the U.S. Copyright Office at http://www.copyright.gov.
10. Ritzenthaler, *Preserving Archives and Manuscripts,* 108.
11. For a discussion of book collectors and their idiosyncrasies, see Nicholas A. Basbanes, *Among the Gently Mad: Strategies and Perspectives for the Book-Hunter in the Twenty-first Century* (New York: Henry Holt, 2002).
12. Cowan, "Theft Case."
13. The ACRL's Rare Books and Manuscript Section's Security Committee keeps a list of thefts at http://www.rbms.nd.edu/committees/security/theft_reports/index.shtml. You can also submit theft information at this site. Among other organizations that track the theft of cultural objects are the International Council of Museums (http://icom.museum); the International League of Antiquarian Booksellers (http://www.ilab.org); the Antiquarian Booksellers' Association of America, with their Stolen and Missing Books list (http://www.abaa.org/cgi-bin/abaa/databases/stolen_search.html); and the Ligue des Bibliothèques Européennes de Recherche (http://www.libereurope.eu/node/163). The Antiquarian Booksellers' Association of America also offers a stolen book alert service. The National Archives and Records Administration's program titled Help the National Archives Recover Lost and Stolen Documents seeks information and assistance to recover its materials (see http://www.archives.gov/research/recover/).
14. See note 1 above. For guidelines with regard to materials in special collections and rare book rooms, see the following:

    American Library Association and Society of American Archivists, Joint Committee on Library-Archives Relationships, "ALA-SAA Joint Statement on Access to Original Research Materials," February 1994, http://www.ala.org/ala/acrl/acrlstandards/jointstatement.cfm.

    Association of College and Research Libraries, "Guidelines for Borrowing and Lending Special Collections Materials for Exhibition," January 2005, http://www.ala.org/ala/acrl/acrlstandards/borrowguide.cfm.

Association of College and Research Libraries, "Guidelines for the Security of Rare Books, Manuscripts, and Other Special Collections," July 1999, http://www.ala.org/ala/acrl/acrlstandards/guidelinessecurity.cfm.

Association of College and Research Libraries, "Guidelines on the Selection of General Collection Materials for Transfer to Special Collections," 1999, http://www.ala.org/ala/acrl/acrlstandards/guidelinesselection.cfm.

Association of College and Research Libraries, "Guidelines Regarding Thefts in Libraries," January 2003, http://www.ala.org/ala/acrl/acrlstandards/guidelinesregardingthefts.cfm.

Association of College and Research Libraries, "Standards for Ethical Conduct for Rare Book, Manuscript, and Special Collections Librarians: With Guidelines for Institutional Practice in Support of the Standards," 2nd ed., 1994, http://www.rbms.nd.edu/standards/code_of_ethics.shtml. ("Standards for Ethical Conduct for Rare Book, Manuscript, and Special Collections Librarians" first appeared in 1987 and was designed to amplify and supplement the ALA Code of Ethics. A second edition of the standards was approved by the ACRL in 1993. This version, recast as a simplified "Code of Ethics for Special Collections Librarians" with commentary, was approved by the ACRL in October 2003.)

15. For more information on disaster response, consult Conservation OnLine, "Disaster Preparedness and Response," http://palimpsest.stanford.edu/bytopic/disasters/; and Miriam B. Kahn, *Disaster Response and Planning for Libraries,* 2nd ed. (Chicago: American Library Association, 2002).

Chapter 6

Security for Art, Objects, and Exhibits

Libraries, archives, historical societies, and museums display parts of their collections as exhibits all the time. The location of the exhibits depends on the type of institution and the purpose of the exhibit. Usually, the more valuable, rare, and unique materials are on display inside the special collections and archives reading rooms. These exhibits are open for viewing when the building's collections are open to the public. Materials from the circulating collections or of general interest are displayed in many areas of libraries and archives. They could be in the halls or scattered among the circulating collections. These displays are more vulnerable to theft and mutilation by the general public if the public corridors are accessible after the collections close. These halls and corridors are in public areas where there are meeting rooms and restrooms that can be accessed by patrons when the collections are closed and staff members have gone home for the night.

SURVEYING THE EXHIBIT AND DISPLAY AREAS

When you survey the inside of the building, you want to note any problem spots in the public areas of the building. Indicate on your floor plan where the public entrances are and where the various exhibits and displays are located. Carefully note any display areas that lie outside the flow of traffic. These are vulnerable areas and should be monitored by security guards or cameras. Check for alarm systems on cases and confirm that they ring in the security office. (See the checklist "Exhibitions" in appendix A.)

Check the security or locks on the exhibit cases and cabinets to confirm that they are locked at the beginning and end of each day. Confirm that the security alarm system is active and the environment is acceptable. Exhibit particularly rare or valuable materials in cases that have alarm systems hardwired into the security system. The cases should be wired for changes in temperature, for particulate matter, for glass breakage, and for movement. All display cases should be secured to the walls or anchored to the floor. Rare or valuable materials that are displayed in frames on the wall should be affixed so that they are difficult to remove, and they should be wired into the alarm system to prevent theft. You might consider attaching RFID or microdots to valuable artwork (particularly for items that are listed on your insurance policy) in order to be able to identify them in case of theft.[1] Security cameras should monitor these exhibition areas, as should motion detectors and smoke detectors.

KEEPING TRACK OF COLLECTIONS

Develop an inventory control system for all items on exhibit, following the recommendations of the ACRL and the National Park Service's *Museum Handbook*.[2] Paper and photographic materials on exhibit should be treated just the same as artwork and three-dimensional objects are in this system. The file should contain basic information about each of the items, including the owner, department or lending institution, and monetary value. Give copies of the file to the exhibits curator and to the risk manager to append to the insurance policy. Place a third copy of the inventory with your vital records and valuable papers.

Have a reputable firm appraise the exhibit items. This is especially important if you do not know the current value of the items and you do not have a recent appraisal filed with the provenance papers or in your catalog. If an item was purchased some time ago or if it was a donation, have it reappraised. Place the appraisal in the file along with the item's provenance. Update your insurance policy and valuable papers or art rider accordingly. Complete the inventory and appraisal prior to exhibiting the items.

Many institutions sponsor exhibits or house objects that belong to other organizations. When you organize an exhibit, it is important to discuss insurance coverage. Lending institutions and organizations should provide insurance for their materials and sign a waiver or release form that holds the hosting institution harmless in the case of damage or theft for the duration of the exhibit. Consult your legal counsel prior to planning a multi-institutional exhibition. (See the "Public Library Exhibitor Release Form" in appendix B.)

If the items are displayed in exhibition cases and cabinets, they should be locked after the materials are placed within to prevent theft. Examine each object before putting it in the case and document any damage or defect. Check the damage against the inventory and description of each item from the lending institution or department. Notify the lending institution if there is damage not noted in the itemized list that accompanies the loaned items. Confirm that all the borrowed items arrived at your institution and that ownership marks are affixed to each object. Document any discrepancies in the file for the exhibit.

Document the terms of the exhibition and its duration, and outline the responsibilities of the host institution. Talk to your legal counsel when drafting contracts or letters of agreement. Some institutions create a database, rather than paper files, for the exhibit, enabling easy access to images, background information, and inventories. This database could be retained after the exhibit is dismantled, or retained to integrate with the online exhibition. You might include information about value, ownership of objects, and the exhibition period. (See the checklist "Exhibit Items on Loan from Other Departments or Institutions" in appendix A.)

Do not place exhibited materials that could be damaged or destroyed by water under sprinkler heads and water pipes. Materials that are susceptible to damage from light should not be exhibited for longer than three months. If the materials are destined to be exhibited for longer than three months, consider having a facsimile created. If this is not possible, consider rotating a number of similar items into the exhibit. Consult with the preservation and special collections/archives staff members before mounting an exhibit of light-sensitive or fragile materials.

TRANSPORTING COLLECTIONS

When mounting an exhibition that includes works of art and three-dimensional objects from other institutions, it may be necessary to hire professional shippers, packers, and exhibition installers. Use formal letters of agreement when borrowing or lending materials for exhibition. (See the form "Special Permission Loan Agreement" in appendix B.) Discuss and agree upon appropriate environmental and physical conditions for the duration of the exhibit. Specify in writing any special requirements for packing, handling, and shipping materials that are sent from one institution to another for exhibition. Depending on the value and fragility of the materials lent or borrowed, conservators or curators may handle and install the objects for exhibition. See the ACRL guidelines for exhibitions of special collections.[3]

There are times when you will exhibit materials in other departments or buildings within your institution. It is still important to document what is being loaned. Place a note in the circulation record and in the provenance file, and most especially in the files that normally house the collections. Indicate the duration of the loan (beginning and ending dates) and the person and department responsible for accepting and returning the materials. The same care and security issues pertain to intra-institutional loans as to inter-institutional ones.

EXHIBITS OFF-SITE

If necessary, visit the host institution to see the physical and environmental conditions in the exhibit area. Learn about the host's security, monitoring, and disaster prevention standards. Include librarians and curators of rare books and special collections departments in discussions about exhibits of fragile, rare, or valuable materials to ensure that these will remain safe in the exhibition cases for the duration of the exhibit.

LOANS

Many medium- and large-size cultural institutions use materials from across their collections for their exhibits. There are times when a special exhibit is created using materials from the special collections, rare books, and archives departments. Items from these special collections can be rare, valuable, or fragile. Quite often they are unique. Whether the materials are loaned from another department within the institution or from another institution, their locations must be tracked. In chapter 5 we discussed identification marks and accession files for special collections, as well as creating temporary catalog records so the department knows where each item is at any given time.

Some institutions take digital photographs of the front and back of each item as a quick or on-the-fly method of creating a "catalog" or inventory. In this way, every item leaving a collection where materials do not traditionally circulate is identified. It is important to note changes in the location of these exhibit items as they move across campus or into temporary storage.

The loan policies for special collections, archives, rare books, and manuscript collections should specify types of appropriate use, duration, renewal period, and the quantity of items loaned at any one time to one location. This loan policy is even more important when parts of these unique collections are loaned within the institution.

The special collections department staff should work with the preservation and conservation staff when determining which materials to put on exhibit. Exhibits are often the catalyst for additional processing and cataloging. At the same time, the materials should be examined to determine if they require stabilization and conservation treatment. If an object is deemed too fragile for exhibition, you might consider creating a facsimile that represents the object and is more durable than the original. Document all preservation and conservation decisions. This is especially important when postponement of treatment until after the exhibition's conclusion is indicated.

In the same way that you change your records of the location of special collections items when they are on exhibit, you will want to indicate if they are going to be in the preservation and conservation department for treatment. Keep a record of the proposed work in the file, along with the date the item was sent for conservation and the amount of time the repairs should take. If you are sending an item to a conservation facility, add the same information to the file along with documentation about the insurance. (See the "Conservation Transmittal Form" in appendix B.)

When items are returned from loan, the special collections staff should check that everything was returned. Examine the materials to make certain there is no damage as a result of handling and exhibition. Document any physical changes and compare them with the photographs taken beforehand. If you exhibit photographs or other materials that are light-sensitive, such as maps, drawings, and blueprints, make a note for the file so that the same items are not selected for the next exhibit.

Part of preparing and selecting materials for exhibition includes reviewing or reinforcing existing policies for lending and borrowing materials. You will want to consider the protocols for duplication of materials while on loan after confirming copyright ownership. Included in the review of your institution's loan policy should be guidelines for the duration of loans, the maximum allowable numbers of items lent or borrowed, and which staff member(s) within the rare books, special collections, and archives departments can authorize loans.

PROTECTING LOANED ITEMS

When loaning your materials or collections to other institutions or departments, it is essential to document

- what is being sent (i.e., a specific inventory with indication of loan in the cataloging record for the collection, any damage, and identifying markings or property stamps)
- where the materials are going
- who is in charge of the exhibit, along with their contact information
- the environmental conditions the materials are usually housed in, and what the conditions at the borrowing institution will be like
- the duration of the loan

Confirm that everything sent on loan has a file describing its physical attributes and makeup, photographs or digital images, provenance, and insurance. Duplicate the information and store it off-site or in a separate location. Indicate the loan in the circulation record and include the date sent and where the object was sent, along with emergency contact information and anticipated date of return. (See the checklist "Loans: Intra-institutional or Inter-institutional" in appendix A.)

Notes

1. Chaptman, "Tag—You're IDed," talks about the concept of tracking inventory with RFID for businesses. RFID is currently being used in security tags in books at some libraries. The Kent Free Library in Kent, Ohio, for one, started installing them in 2005.
2. National Park Service, Museum Management Program, *Museum Handbook* (Washington, DC: Government Printing Office, 2006), http://www.nps.gov/history/museum/publications/handbook.html.
3. Association of College and Research Libraries, "Guidelines for Borrowing and Lending Special Collections Materials for Exhibition," http://www.ala.org/ala/acrl/acrlstandards/borrowguide.cfm.

Chapter

7 Security for Local and Remote Storage Facilities

Storage areas are so commonplace in libraries, archives, museums, and historical societies that we hardly think of them as places with security and safety risks. Each type of cultural institution uses storage areas differently. Libraries tend to use theirs for storing little-used materials, older reference works, back runs of journals, and, in some cases, materials where there is no room in that department.

Rare book and special collections house the majority of their collections in nonpublic areas that could be far from their reading rooms. Less-requested or low-use materials might be stored on another floor or in a locked area in a secured storage room on the premises. The most valuable items are stored in vaults, safes, or locked areas within the stacks.

Historical societies and archives tend to use storage areas for unprocessed collections, seldom-used materials, and bulky three-dimensional items. Materials with restricted access or that are temporarily sealed are also often kept in storage areas. Depending on the size of the institution, all nonprint materials might be shelved in storage areas separate from the print or paper-based collections. If there are institutional archives, the confidential materials and less-used items are placed in storage areas. But items with historical value or those requested frequently should be kept where they are easily retrievable.

As a rule, museums house between 75 and 90 percent of their art objects in storage areas, and rotate their collections depending on interest and gallery space. The storage area of the library in the museum tends to house lesser-used materials, including older journals and reference materials that support research about objects not currently on display.

Storage areas are usually not the same as closed stacks areas. Closed stacks areas are generally near reading rooms and are for active, regularly used materials. Storage areas tend to be separate from the main collections, perhaps in a basement or in another building on the grounds of the institution.

The materials stored in other buildings are often retrieved only when requested by patrons or staff. This also means that when a staff member goes to retrieve the items, there may not be anyone else around. The safety of the staff member who is sent to the storage area is important, as is the security of the stored items.

SURVEYING THE STORAGE AREA

Survey the storage area to determine what potential security and safety risks exist. (See the checklist "Storage Areas" in appendix A.) Take a look at all the entrances into the area. Do you enter the storage area from outside the building or from within? If you enter from without, is there a light above the door? Is it triggered by motion or darkness? How much of the area does the light illuminate? Is the staff person required to walk up or down stairs to get to the door and if so, are these stairwells well lit? Do the buildings and grounds staff keep the stairs clean of debris and obstructions, particularly in bad weather? Is the area lighted to prevent injury? Does the door require a key or a key card? Who has copies of the keys?

If you enter the storage area from the inside of the building, is a key required to access that floor from the elevator or stairwell? Is there a way to exit the floor without a key? For security and fire safety reasons, exit doors should open from the inside without a key. An alarm should ring any time an emergency door opens. Does this inside entrance door require a key or a key code? If so, how does the staff person get access? Is there lighting in the hallway? If so, how is it activated?

Does the maintenance staff clean this storage area? When are they given access to the area and by whom? A staff member should be present to monitor the cleaning staff's activities to prevent damage or loss to the collection. Set up a cleaning schedule during regular working hours. If you have a regular schedule for retrieving items from storage, you might schedule cleaning at those times.

Talk to the security department to find out when they patrol the storage area. Do the guards go into the rooms or just patrol the perimeter of the building and the external hallways? Are the guards who patrol the storage area the same as those who work with the library or archive, or are they ones responsible for the host building? If the storage area is in a separate building, do the security staff members know who to call if there is a disaster (fire or water) or if there is evidence of a burglary such as open or broken doors? During the meeting with the security staff, establish criteria for when to contact the library or archive staff or the person in charge of the building itself. Ask the disaster response team leader to join you at this meeting. If there are different administrators responsible for the building and the collections, establish protocols to prevent a breakdown in communications when there is a problem in the storage area. This is essential when there is a disaster. Define who is responsible for what within the storage area. At first glance, there should be a firm line between responsibility for the building and for the collections stored in the storage area. Some flexibility is called for, however, especially if the problem or disaster affects both the building and the stored materials. Try to work out this division of responsibility before trouble strikes.

SECURITY

Look to see if there is a camera above the entrance so the security guards can keep track of who is entering and exiting the storage area. Is the camera activated by motion, or is it always on? Does the camera record the activity onto tape, or does it just show the guard what is happening? If it records, find out how long until the tape or disc is overwritten with new images. Ask if the images can be stored or moved to another location in case of a break-in. During your meeting, determine which security station is responsible for monitoring access to the storage area: the library or archive, or the host building?

Talk to the security staff about preventing unauthorized access, especially after hours. For example, if there is a mechanical room in the storage area, then someone from the facilities maintenance, security, or library or archive staff should be present when a contractor is servicing this equipment. If this is a "secure" or locked storage area for special collections, then staff may want to be present when any work, maintenance, cleaning, or servicing is performed in this area. If a staff member is not present, then a member of the security staff must be.

SURVEYING INSIDE THE STORAGE AREA

Once inside the storage area, how is the lighting activated? Is there a switch just inside the doorway, or is the light activated by motion or when the door is opened? How long do the lights stay on and how do they turn off? The light switch should never be on the outside of the room unless the lights are activated by key. This is to prevent the lights being shut off when someone is inside.

There should be an emergency phone or call box inside the storage area in case a staff member is injured or needs assistance. Install an emergency alarm or panic button that can be triggered from various locations in the storage area. The farther away the storage area is from the main building, the more need for alarms and security cameras.

Look for the emergency exit. There should be a map posted near the entrance showing the nearest emergency exit. Post a second map inside the entrance showing the route to the emergency exit when inside the storage area. There should be an emergency exit from the storage area that is separate from the keyed entrance door. Can you see the exit sign from various places in the storage area? Can you see the emergency exit sign if the lights are off? The emergency exit door should lead outside the storage area without permitting reentry. Ask the same questions about emergency exits from the storage area as from the main building: Where does the emergency exit lead? Is there a stairwell or hallway to traverse before exiting the building? You should not be able to reenter the storage area from the emergency stairwell or hallway.

You should be able to hear and see the emergency alarm and warning system when inside the storage area. The safety lights should activate when the power goes off, and they should illuminate enough of the area so anyone inside can exit safely. Check to see where the flashlights and batteries are located. There should be a number of them located throughout the storage area.

Staff safety within the storage area is equally important. Are there a sufficient number of ladders or footstools so that the staff member can retrieve the requested materials without injury? Does retrieval of items from the storage area require two people? If there are lots of heavy boxes that require ladders to reach them or lots of lifting to move them around, an emergency alarm is even more important to alert security to injury. Of course, the storage area should be included in the disaster response plan for the library or archive and the building itself, especially if it is in a location separate from the main collections.

TRANSPORTING MATERIALS TO STORAGE

The third aspect of safety and security for the storage area is the method of transport available to move items from the storage area to the main building or reference area. Do the staff members retrieving storage materials carry the items or push them on a cart? Can you move the requested items on a cart to the elevator and then across the institution's campus to the main building? What do you do in inclement weather? If there is a branch of the library or archive in the building where the storage area is located, materials could be brought to that particular reading room or reference area for patrons to consult, especially if those particular items do not circulate. If the latter is the case, discuss how and under what circumstances storage items are transported to a branch library. Review the standard security procedures to ensure appropriate care and handling of these storage items. If establishing and enforcing separate use procedures at the branch library is burdensome for the staff, then have the materials brought to the special collections or archives reading room directly.

SECURITY FOR THE COLLECTION

There are several issues to discuss in detail with the manager of the building where the storage area is located. The last thing you want is to have an argument over territorial issues when both of you want to protect the building and whatever is housed within it. Talk over the issues listed below and work out a cooperative arrangement that involves active communication and a plan for dealing with issues of theft, unauthorized access, security, and "disaster" (fire or water) ahead of time.

Here are some questions to ask and consider:

Cleaning. Does the cleaning staff clean this storage area? Does the cleaning staff work for the building where the storage area is located, or for the library or archive? When and how are they given access to the storage area? If the cleaning staff works for the building, then there should be a library staff member or a security guard present when they are in the storage area. If the cleaning staff works for the library, it is a good idea to have them clean when someone from the library or archive staff is present. This is a good security measure to prevent loss or damage to the collections. It is even more important if the cleaning staff are contract employees.

Security guards. Do the security guards patrol the building housing the storage area? Do they patrol inside the storage area? Or do they patrol the perimeter of the storage area, including all hallways, and around the outside of the building itself? How often do they patrol? The security guards should come by several times during the period the building is closed. It is important to review with the security guards which department or staff members are called in case of an emergency. This is even more important if the library or archive storage area is housed and accessible through another building.

Staff notification. Under what circumstances is the building manager called, and when are the library or archive staff called? You need to work with the building manager to determine how various problems will be handled and by whom. For instance, the building manager is called if there are broken windows or doors, and the library or archive staff is called if the damage is to the storage area. Both would get calls for fire. If there is water on the floor, then the department where the water is located gets the call, unless it is dripping or pouring from the ceiling.

Entrances and exits. Are there additional entrances or exits providing access to the collection without using the main door? What about the windows? The elevator? And stairways? There should be alarms that alert the security department that there are open or broken windows. All windows that are below grade and at ground level should have bars or gates with alarms attached to them. Any doors that are opened without keys or the appropriate code should ring alarms in the security office. A security guard should check out the alarm immediately.

SAFETY FOR PEOPLE

Is the storage area staffed at all hours or only when there is a request for an item? If the storage area is staffed during all the hours the building or library is open, it is common practice to have at least two staff members present at all times for both safety and security reasons. This is to protect both the staff members and the collection. If there is only one staff member at all times, consider having someone cover during breaks, meals, and meetings. Another staff member should also be available to cover on sick days and vacations. Install an emergency buzzer so the staff member can call for help.

If the materials are retrieved on a schedule or upon request, no staff member should go to the storage area without someone knowing where he or she is. If possible, send two people to retrieve materials, again for both safety and security reasons. The staff who retrieve materials should know who to call in an emergency (fire, flood, injury, theft, broken windows or doors), and they should know where the emergency phone, alarms, and exits are located. They should never let anyone who is not on the library or archive staff into the storage area to help them retrieve materials.

How does the library or archive limit who can gain access to the storage area? What procedures are in place to prevent unauthorized access? Do you train your staff to be alert when they are entering and leaving the storage area? Just as they should not let any nonstaff member in the storage area to help retrieve materials, they should be certain to lock the door upon exiting. Never leave the door propped open while retrieving materials from the storage area. You never know who could wander in.

For the safety of your staff, there should be emergency alarms or panic buttons located in strategic places within the storage area in case of trouble or injury. Of course, the emergency lighting should be connected to a generator or battery backup in case of a power outage. Emergency exit signage should illuminate when there is no power. You might consider fluorescent signs in case the backup generator fails. Check the emergency evacuation alarm and notification system to confirm that it can be heard and seen in the storage area. Confirm that the alarm system and security system for the storage area are on the emergency power grid.

Is there a reading area or circulation function at the storage area? If so, who confirms that materials are not removed without checking out the items? Who watches the users in this reading area? If there is a reading room associated with the storage area, then there should be at least one staff member in the area at all times. At no time should both staff members be on a break or retrieving materials. Someone must always watch the reading room and take care of the circulation functions. When closing for the night, the procedures should include checking the area for patrons who were using the reading area in order to confirm that they did leave. Restrooms should be readily accessible for those using reading rooms. The public should never enter the storage area to enter, exit, or use the restrooms.

Remember, the storage areas are out of sight, as are the collections. This means that security guards should patrol the area with some frequency to discourage theft and vandalism. If materials in the storage area are requested on a very irregular basis, then someone on the staff should be assigned to go there on a regular basis (weekly at the very least) to check that the doors and windows are secure, the environment is stable, and there is no water damage, standing water, or any other type of damage to the collections.

COMMERCIAL RECORD STORAGE FACILITIES

Some archives will store materials at a commercial record storage facility. Traditionally, institutional records that have a limited life span (five to seven years) with a scheduled destruction date would be stored at a commercial record facility. However, commercial facilities such as Iron Mountain National Underground Storage (www.ironmountain.com) house materials of a permanent nature that require a very controlled environment. These materials include photographs, master microfilm, provenance records for museums and artists, and other collections of a permanent yet seldom-retrieved nature. It is essential that commercial storage facilities have a disaster response plan and security to prevent the theft of materials in their care.

Talk to the manager of the commercial storage facility and ask about their security arrangements and precautions, as well as a disaster response plan. Your institution should have only one or two locations the materials can be sent to and specified staff who request and retrieve materials.

Ask about the disaster response plan at the commercial record storage facility and make certain they have contact information for the authorized staff member at your institution. Ask if they are a member of PRISM International and if they meet that association's standards as a record storage facility.[1] If the record storage company has no security in place or if they are unwilling to discuss their security measures and standards with you, then look for another facility.

REMOTE STORAGE FACILITIES AND DEPOSITORIES

Over the last twenty years, cultural institutions have built remote depositories that are located some distance from the library or archive. Some remote storage depositories serve a number of institutions or a consortium in a geographical area. Others serve only a specific institution.

Remote storage depositories are built specifically for the high-density storage of books and archival materials with environmental controls and no overhead water pipes. Some storage depositories are physically attached to their institution's archive. In this case, the storage depository should have separate environmental controls and security from the reading rooms, staff offices, and processing areas.

Remote storage depositories are built like warehouses with twenty-foot-high stacks and use mechanical equipment to access the collections. Materials are requested through interlibrary or intralibrary loan. Items are shipped to other libraries from the remote storage depository, requiring care when handling and retrieving. Circulation system access or inventory control is also necessary to be able to identify what has been loaned out and what is in the depository.

Just as a remote storage depository requires a disaster response plan, so it is important to take a look at security and safety issues for these buildings. Begin as you did with the library or archive buildings by examining the outside for security and safety problems. (See the checklist "Storage Areas" in appendix A.)

Surveying the Remote Storage Depository

Walk around the outside of the depository and note where the emergency exit doors and loading dock doors are. Are there emergency exit doors that cannot be seen from the main entrance, the road, or the loading docks? If so, how are the doors secured? Is there an alarm system? Do you use a key card, keypad, or regular key to open the door from the outside? Is there a handle on the outside of the door? You want to ensure that there is no easy access to the remote storage depository from these unseen emergency exits. Even more important, you want to protect those working inside from unauthorized visitors.

Look at all the emergency exit doors. Do these doors open at ground level, or do you have to climb stairs? If there are stairs, are they kept clean of obstructions, debris, and ice or snow in the bad weather months? Is there a light near the door? If so, is it on during evening hours, or on a timer, or is it activated by a motion detector? Is there a security camera and if so, how is it activated and who monitors the camera?

Continue your walk around the outside of the building and make a note of the location of the fresh-air intake. Is it closed and secured against unauthorized access? The grate should be locked to prevent someone from falling through it and to prevent someone from gaining access to the building. Is there anything obstructing the intake of fresh air? Remove any debris and check the intake periodically. Are there lots of plantings around the fresh-air intake where a person could hide while waiting for the building to empty at night? If so, remove or trim the plantings.

Now take a look at the loading dock. How does the driver gain access to the collections or the materials waiting for pickup? Is there a bell, intercom system, or phone that rings at the security or supervisor's desk? Is there a security camera with a monitor placed where the person who opens the door to the loading dock can see who is out there? Are there specific hours that deliveries are made and shipped out? If so, there should be no fewer than two people in the facility at all times. The same security system in place at the main library or archive should be in place at the remote storage depository. Design a separate security plan as well as a disaster response plan for this facility. Keep these plans together and send a copy for inclusion in the institution's disaster or emergency response plan.

Safety and Security Issues

Remote storage depositories are usually run with a minimum number of people, so it is important to think about the safety of the staff working in the building. Just as there is security for those staff members retrieving materials from a storage area on the institution's grounds, the same is necessary at the remote storage depository, and even more so if the depository is located in a rural area.

The remote storage depository should be equipped with emergency alarms and panic buttons in case of injury or intrusion. The alarms should ring at the local police station as well as at the security department of the closest institutional member. Talk with the police and security departments and establish protocols and procedures for responding to any emergency alarms. Also discuss who to notify in an emergency. All of this information should be added to the disaster response plan.

Of course, there should be signs pointing the way to emergency exits. Emergency lighting should be wired into battery backup or an emergency generator in case of a power outage. Fire alarms and emergency alert systems should be audible and visible throughout the remote storage depository. All security systems, security cameras, and alarm systems must be wired to the emergency power grid.

Policies should be in place to record, prevent, and investigate unauthorized access or after-hours access. Because remote storage depositories retrieve materials for use at the home institution or for interlibrary loan, there is no need for staff in the building after the workday is over, unless the facility also houses the archives or special collections. In that case, there should be a clear delineation between the parts of the building used by staff for the remote storage depository and those used for the archives, and there should be no access to the storage areas after the working day is over.

If there is a reading room at the remote storage depository, the staff members working in that room should monitor the materials' use and the patrons using the collection. Just as the users of the special collections, rare books, and archives on the institution's grounds are monitored, so too at the remote storage depository. Have lockers for coats and belongings readily available and locate restrooms nearby. The door between the reading room and the remote storage depository should be locked at all times and the security alarm activated at the end of the working day. The door between the two areas should never be propped open, for this is a fire hazard and a security risk.

Staff retrieving materials from the depository should be trained to handle these items carefully to prevent damage from dropping and inappropriate shelving practices. Just as collections are monitored and controlled to prevent loss at the institution, so supervisors should monitor the actions of staff members to prevent theft and mutilation of materials at the depository. When journal articles are requested for interlibrary loan, trained personnel should copy or scan the materials to prevent damage to these possibly fragile items. Ask the preservation department or special collections department librarian to train the remote storage depository staff in proper handling procedures for brittle materials.

Always arrange for the remote storage depository to be cleaned during working hours. If this is not possible, then arrange for security to monitor the actions of the cleaning staff. The same goes for maintenance of the mechanical equipment. If contractors are working at the remote depository, then there must be a staff member or security guard present. Never give contractors access to the security codes so they can work on equipment at night!

Note

1. PRISM (Professional Records and Information Services Management) International, http://www.prismintl.org, "is a trade association for companies that provide their clients with protection, access, retention, storage and disposal of their vital information."

Chapter 8

Security for Computer Equipment, Electronic Data, and Websites

In this chapter we will focus on protecting the computers themselves from physical damage and theft. Then we will review, in a very general way, securing data, catalogs, and databases from hackers and malicious mischief. It is important to protect institutional computer systems from people who want to change data and websites, or plant viruses and other damaging programs. Lastly, we will take a brief look at using software to protect children from accessing inappropriate websites. Each of these topics is a book unto itself, so my aim is to provide an overview and some preventive measures to protect the computer resources that are integral to providing effective services for all users.

Just as you surveyed the building for exits and potential breaches to the security and safety of your institution's collections and staff members, now you will look at each floor. You want to indicate on the plan where the computers are located and how vulnerable they are to theft. Start with the public areas of each floor. Draw the computer locations onto your map, indicating the computers that are at reference and information desks, the ones that contain public online catalogs, and those the public can use for Internet access, word processing, and data design. Survey all the departments in your library, archive, historical society, or museum. Don't forget information kiosks and directional computers.

Once you have finished surveying the public areas, move to the staff areas and indicate on your map where all the other computers are located. Include computers in workrooms, offices, and the IT department. Make a note of the types of computers in conference and training rooms. Indicate if they are portable or desktop computers. List the types and quantities of computer peripheral equipment located in each of these staff areas. Don't forget to indicate the types of computer equipment in the server and network rooms.

If you have a portable or wireless classroom, make a notation on your floor plan as to where these items are stored when not in use. The cabinet or cart that holds the portable classroom should be locked, the laptops secured inside the cart, and the cart secured in a storage room or to a wall when not in use.

Coordinate this survey or inventory of computers with the computer or IT disaster response team. As part of their plan, the information technology or information systems department has an inventory of all computer equipment, peripherals, operating systems, software, and specialized programs, as well as a schedule for backup of the data and maintenance of the equipment. For more information on this topic, look at books on contingency planning.[1]

It is important to identify potential risks to your computer equipment. As part of your disaster response plan, you want to locate computers and peripherals away from water pipes, radiators, and air-handling ducts. This will prevent damage to the hardware from water, excessive heat, and particulate matter. It is possible to dry, clean, and recertify water-damaged computer hardware, but it is simpler to protect the equipment.

SECURING YOUR COMPUTERS

Let's start with theft prevention. You want to physically secure the equipment so it cannot be stolen. In many cases this means anchoring the hard drive, monitor, and keyboard, as well as the mouse, to the table. It is very common to secure laptops (especially in portable classrooms) to the table. Other institutions use some type of locking mechanism to secure the hardware to the table. Some keyboards come with a trackball attached to the front or side. If you have had damage or theft of mice, you might consider purchasing an all-in-one keyboard. On the other hand, some institutions use older models of computers or those with less functionality for their public access terminals. In this case, the institution may not physically secure its computer monitors and keyboards. This means that security guards and circulation desk staff should stop and question anyone walking out of the building with desktop computer components. Security guards in archives, historical societies, and special collections and rare book departments should monitor those who enter and leave with laptop computers and peripheral equipment.

Computer equipment in departmental offices and workrooms may be secured to desks. However, you will find that this makes it difficult to rearrange office or work space. If there are many computers in a common work area that is easily accessible from the outside or by patrons, then it is imperative to secure the equipment to prevent theft. If you have computer labs in your building, you will want to physically secure both the hardware and the computer peripherals.

No matter whether you "lock down" your equipment or not, you should physically mark every piece of computer equipment and every peripheral device with institutional property IDs and serial numbers. The IT department keeps a list of the serial numbers for every piece of equipment and its location within the building. These are the same numbers that you use for insurance purposes and maintenance contracts. The inventory list identifies equipment if it is stolen or removed without authorization. Inventorying and marking laptops, printers, LCD projectors, and other types of computer peripherals is even more important, since these items are very portable. Many institutions provide equipment, such as laptops and LCD projectors, for lectures or conferences. IT staff members should routinely secure this equipment to the podium and projection cart for the duration of the presentation or conference.

It is essential to insure the computer equipment against damage and theft. Many institutions have insurance policies protecting against theft of computers above a certain amount of money. If your large office photocopier doubles as a printer, ask the service company about the costs of repair versus replacement. Decide whether this copier-printer is considered a computer peripheral or part of the office equipment and so is covered by that part of the insurance policy. Ask your insurance agent whether the deductible is per piece of equipment or per occurrence. Decide how much the institution can afford to pay to replace stolen or damaged computer equipment, set the deductibles for the insurance policy accordingly, and put emergency funds aside. The other type of insurance policy common for computers is actually a maintenance agreement with the manufacturer or a service provider. In this case, the insurance would cover damage due to failure of a piece of equipment or for service because of software problems and viruses.

SECURING OPERATING SYSTEMS, SOFTWARE, AND DATA

Public Terminals

Some institutions use dedicated terminals for online public access terminals (OPACs). Dedicated computers are networked into a server, so they don't have any need for disk drives and can be programmed to connect to the catalog only. If your institution does not use dedicated terminals for its OPACs, then the IT department should set up the computer so the only program that is accessible is the online catalog. No matter whether patrons turn off or exit the catalog, the only program they can open is the catalog. Any other access to the computer should be password protected, and even that can be at a variety of levels so that the staff can only turn the system on and off and open the public catalog, while the IT staff can access the operating system and change the functionality of terminals and computers.

Patrons should not be able to access any of the operating system or network from public Internet computers. Again, set the computers so that they access only the Web. In addition, have the IT department staff disable many of the menu functions of the computer, thereby limiting patrons' access to internal functions. You can disable not only buttons but also the patrons' ability to bookmark sites. Some institutions permit patrons to bookmark sites they visit, but as soon as the computer is turned off, those bookmarks are erased. Other institutions disable the bookmark function altogether.

There has been much debate over the past ten years about public Internet computers and how much of the Internet library users should be able to access. Some of the discussion centers on blocking websites; another approach involves limiting access to blogs, e-mail, instant messaging, and chat rooms. Establish a policy that describes the extent of access permitted on the public Internet computers as well as appropriate behavior while surfing the Internet at the library.[2]

Children's Departments

Some institutions restrict Internet access in the children's department but not in the rest of the library by using any of a number of website-blocking programs. These policies are designed to protect children from Internet predators and pornography sites. Public libraries have been required to create and enforce these restrictive polices as a prerequisite to receiving federal funding. These requirements, mostly falling under the Communications Decency Act (CDA) and its offshoots, have met with mixed reactions from the public, libraries, and the Supreme Court.[3]

There are two basic types of website-blocking programs: the first blocks websites that contain specific words, while the second blocks websites from lists of sites input by the publisher and the library. Both types of programs are problematic, since they can block sites that contain innocuous research sources.[4] Nevertheless, the Internet blocking programs will prevent users from accessing sites with pornographic materials. They may not necessarily block e-mail or chat rooms. If your institution restricts Internet access, post the policies in prominent locations, including on the institution's website. Staff should have a way to override the website-blocking program when necessary. It might also be necessary to unblock websites during educational training sessions if the instructor and attendees come across unauthorized but useful sites in the course of the seminar.

Computer Labs

Many public and academic libraries and archives have computer labs that contain terminals loaded with programs ranging from basic word processing to sophisticated scanning, drawing, and website design software, along with the associated peripheral equipment. To prevent loss or damage to hardware and damage to software, computer labs should never be without a person staffing the room. These labs are usually monitored by someone with enough expertise to troubleshoot patrons' problems.

Access to more than the programs should be restricted. In other words, the users should never be able to access the network, server, or intranet. Limiting access to programs only restricts patrons from changing and accessing the computer networks and data, and thereby protects the software and operating systems. Again, access should be restricted through passwords that limit the administrative capabilities of the computer lab technicians. The administrative level should enable only the limited manipulation of some software.

Establish policies about downloading and installing software and data. Some institutions prohibit the installation of any software by users, especially from the Internet. This is a good policy because it decreases the chance of inadvertently installing a virus, worm, or Trojan horse. Other institutions set their software so that every time it is turned off or rebooted, the system resets itself to a set configuration. This is very common in computer training labs, where participants can learn a variety of techniques and install software and bookmarks. At the end of the session, the computer reverts to its original image or configuration.

Some institutions limit the amount of time patrons can actually use their computers. This is accomplished in three different ways. The first is to have patrons sign up for specific computers so that the staff must monitor the user's time. Another is to have the computers automatically shut down and reboot after a specific period of time, ranging from half an hour to an hour. Of course, there is nothing to stop a patron from going to another terminal or another building and using another computer until it too shuts down. The final method of limiting access time is based upon library card number. This method requires a user to have a valid card and to use the card to activate the public Internet or computer lab equipment. At the same time, the library card usually serves as a debit card to pay for any copies printed during that session. If computer sessions are limited by library card, provisions need to be made for patrons without cards. The reference or information desk staff could have guest library cards to hand out. Again, the institution needs to publish its policy concerning limiting time on computers.[5] Limiting time on public Internet terminals decreases the number of patrons who come to the library and monopolize the computers.

Staff Computers

The computers that are on reference, circulation, and information desks should be password protected so that only authorized staff members can access the internal databases and the circulation system. A limited number of people should have access or passwords permitting them to modify library card accounts and update or change circulation records. If someone from the general public uses an information desk computer, he should not be able to get onto the computer network or into data files. In fact, you might consider having two modes: one that is password protected that permits limited access to the network server, and one that accesses only the catalog reference databases and basic circulation system functions for issuing library cards and for checking books in and out of the library.

Office Computers

Staff or nonpublic-area computers should also be password protected. This is especially important if the computers use software and data mounted on a shared server or network. Staff capabilities and access can be limited by their passwords and by their administrative level within a server or network system. It is common for IT staff members to have fairly broad access and for staff to have more limited capabilities. This prevents a disgruntled employee from planting a virus or Trojan horse in the circulation system, website, or online catalog. Of course, it would not restrict an unhappy IT staff member from doing the same.

Earlier we discussed changing passwords and access when staff members leave or are terminated. This ensures that former employees cannot access your internal computers, data systems, and websites. This prevents malicious mischief and outright destruction of computer networks. If your institution has intranets, "secret" IP addresses, and backdoor access methods via the Internet or a modem, all these passwords should be changed and carefully monitored when a staff member leaves.

In the normal course of business and operations, the security and IT departments should monitor the computer networks closely to prevent unauthorized access by hackers who may be curious or malicious, and by those who would install viruses and spyware. The IT department staff members should send out regular reminders to employees about the dangers of downloading items from unknown persons, in order to prevent inadvertent access to computers through phishing, e-mail, and viruses. The IT department should install antivirus software on all computers, update the software regularly, and scan systems routinely. They should teach staff members to scan their desktop and laptop computers, as well as any removable data storage devices, for viruses. The last is even more important in the public computer labs that permit users to bring in their own portable or removable storage devices. If this becomes a serious issue, the institution may need to require all users of public computer labs to purchase portable storage devices from the lab.

Some institutions discourage their staff from downloading and installing unauthorized software programs onto their desktop computers. This policy is undertaken in response to two dangers. The first is the inadvertent contraction of a virus, worm, or Trojan horse. The second is that if staff members do not routinely back up their data onto either the network or a removable storage device, and their hard drive is corrupted or fails, the IT department will install a new configuration and all previous data and downloaded programs will be lost. This policy also prevents the installation of pirated or unlicensed software.

Firewalls are essential for computer networks to prevent hackers and minimize viruses. If your institution has Wi-Fi (wireless fidelity) Internet access for users and staff, it is imperative that there should be security on the network. You want a firewall between public user access and staff computers or the institution's network. User names and passwords are the norm, and encryption is important, especially if the institution wants to limit who has access. If there is no security on a Wi-Fi network, then it will have unauthorized users.[6] It is not unusual for a library or archive to provide guest accounts for users who do not have cards or are visitors to the community. As a security measure, you might want to have the guest account passwords expire after a day or a week.

The only way to prevent someone from hacking into your systems is to isolate computers from the network and the Internet. The most sensitive information should reside on computers in this type of isolated network. Otherwise, passwords, encryption, and firewalls are your best protection. The tighter your security, the less likely you are to have unauthorized users.

Notes

1. There are many books on the subject of contingency planning, or protecting your company and computers from loss of data. Books and articles on protecting data from loss can be found under the Library of Congress subject headings of Computer Security, Emergency Management Planning, and Data Protection, or under natural language phrases such as Contingency Planning or Business Contingency Planning.
2. For more information on this topic, consult articles on the CDA (which is part of the Telecommunications Act of 1996) and the Children's Internet Protection Act (CIPA). The ALA provides information and sample policies on its website at http://www.ala.org/ala/washoff/woissues/civilliberties/cipaweb/cipa.cfm.
3. Other federal acts or restrictions include CIPA, the Children's Online Protection Act (COPA), and the Child Pornography Protection Act (CPPA). See the ALA website at http://www.ala.org/ala/oif/ifissues/issuesrelatedlinks/cppacopacipa.cfm.
4. For more about this and other issues that affect intellectual freedom, see the ALA's coverage of intellectual freedom at http://www.ala.org/ala/oif/ifissues/.
5. A policy for limiting time for use of computers can be found at the Columbus (Ohio) Metropolitan Library's website in the "About Us" section under "Frequently Asked Questions: Computers in the Library," http://columbuslibrary.org/ebranch/index.cfm?pageid=26#7.
6. Marshall Breeding, "Wireless Networks Connect Libraries to a Mobile Society," *Computers in Libraries* 24, no. 9 (October 2004): 29–31.

Chapter

9 Property and Casualty Insurance

All libraries, archives, museums, and historical societies should have insurance policies that cover their collections and other contents of their buildings. Even very large institutions that are self-insured, that is, that pay for their losses from their own budgets, may have an insurance policy that can be drawn upon when there is a catastrophic loss. In many cases, these large institutions have a very high deductible tied into state or city insurance policies or into emergency funding.

Your institution may have a number of insurance policies or riders; some cover health, others cover the facility or campus, and still others cover the library, archive, and art collections. Some institutions have an overall insurance policy that deals with both property and casualty. This is the one you are looking for. The property/casualty policy includes all the physical objects within the library, archive, or museum, including the books, furniture, and equipment. Review the policy and see that the library, archive, or special collections are named, and determine what the limitations and deductibles are. (See the checklist "Insurance" in appendix A.)

Insurance policies for the collections held in libraries, archives, museums, or historical societies vary in complexity. Each insurance policy covers collections differently, so it is important to review the insurance coverage on a regular basis, say at least every other year. It is even more important to review the policy when your parent institution changes insurance carriers.

Special riders can be purchased to cover parts of the collection such as artwork and rare books. Additional short-term riders should be purchased when the need arises, such as a special exhibition or when part of the collection is transported from one location to another, or even if part of your collection is stored off-site while the building is under renovation.[1]

Purchase insurance for the collections from firms that specialize in commercial insurance coverage and, when possible, that specialize in insuring cultural institutions. It is essential that the insurance agent understand what the needs of the library or archive are and be able to provide appropriate coverage. Jeanne Drewes provides a selected list of "Insurance Companies with Cultural Institution Policies" on the Library of Congress's Preservation Office website under "Emergency Preparedness, Insurance/Risk Management" (http://www.loc.gov/preserv/emergprep/insurancemain.html). Other lists of insurance companies that specifically insure art collections and exhibitions can be found at www.museumsusa.org in that site's "Vendor Directory."

All insurance polices have limitations to their coverage. There is a deductible and an upper limit to the amount the insurance company will reimburse for loss or damage. In addition, the institution may purchase special riders that vary in length and coverage. All cultural institutions should have insurance on their buildings, contents, and collections. Even if your organization rents space in a building, you must have insurance. Renter's insurance covers the inside part of the building, along with secondary damage and contents.

Issues to consider when purchasing insurance include the following. (Also see the checklist "Establishing Deductible and Contingency Funds for Insurance and Loss" in appendix A.)

How much money can the library cover for each loss?[2] This factors into what types of deductibles and limits you request for your insurance policy. The size of your contingency fund also determines whether you insure for replacement or actual cash value. *Replacement cost* will reimburse the institution for the cost of replacing the material today with the same or a similar item. *Actual cash value* will reimburse you for what the item is worth on the day of the loss. That means if the $200 item is worth $20 today, that's all you get. Be very careful if you select actual cash value because the reimbursement amount may end up being too little money to replace the collections. Ancillary questions to consider when reviewing the insurance policies are the value of the building; the value of the fixtures and furnishings (the carpets, desks, furniture, office equipment, etc.); and what else is located on the physical property. Are there cars or other vehicles housed in the building?

Who or what is at risk of loss?[3] Look at the building's contents and collections. Consider worst-case scenarios as well as common risks. Think about the types of losses and small disasters your institution has suffered in the past. Have the buildings been vandalized? Are there lots of trees around the foundations of the buildings that could damage the building during a storm, hurricane, or tornado? Has the institution embarked on a security campaign where it is installing new locks on doors and windows or is changing locks from keys to electronic devices? Your institution might consider hiring an experienced security consultant to discuss potential risks and to evaluate the quality of the security upgrades being considered and installed.

When was your last review of the costs or value of the collection, especially new acquisitions?[4] Look at how much the collections have increased in quantity. Are you purchasing more of one type of material than another? Perhaps you recently acquired a large donation of valuable materials. Or perhaps you have been adding to your digital collections. Have you discussed these changes to the composition of your collections with your insurance agent? Does the insurance agent consult with the adjusters about the impact of loss of collections upon services? What about potential losses to these specialized collections? Are you purchasing more audiovisual materials? Have you increased the number of computers and peripherals? This review should be performed no less than every other year.

What types of deductions do you receive for preventive measures, such as fire extinguishers, alarms, RFID, sprinklers? Insurance companies and underwriters look at disaster response and emergency response plans to see if they might decrease their potential loss. They are also interested in how your institution plans to decrease the risks to the collections and buildings as a whole. The more prepared you are, the less surprised you will be when a disaster strikes. Security and safety is intertwined with a disaster response plan and concerns staff and administrators alike. Planning is the key to mitigating and reducing loss.

When was the last appraisal of art and rare books/special collections materials?[5] Appraisal includes valuation and provenance. When you have the collections appraised—specifically, works of art, rare books, special collections, and archival collections—you want to look for professional, experienced, and accredited appraisers. You may have to hire more than one appraiser, as they tend to have specialties. If you cannot find one through a reputable used book dealer or professional organization such as the American Institute for Conservation of Historic and Artistic Works, ask your insurance company for a referral. You can also contact the Antiquarian Booksellers' Association of America (www.abaa.org) for a list of their members. Look for a bookseller who specializes in the type of books you need to have appraised or one with lots of experience. Ask for references and check them before hiring.[6] Be certain to insure for the average cost of rare items and the specific cost of unique and extremely valuable items.

What preventive measures against theft, robbery, and damage to rare, special, and general collections and artwork have been enacted since the last insurance policy review? Cultural institutions purchase insurance policies to help pay for the cost of physical damage from natural disasters including fire, flood/water, hurricanes and tornadoes, wind, earthquakes, and other natural causes. In addition, there can be damage from arson, construction, and renovation, as well as negligence. There can also be damage and loss in the aftermath of a natural disaster or disruption in power (which has an effect upon the institution's infrastructure). It is not uncommon for there to be looting and malicious damage to businesses and cultural institutions after a hurricane or tornado. A widespread power outage, when electronic surveillance and security may be compromised, is another time when looting, theft, and damage can occur.

THE PARTS OF AN INSURANCE POLICY

Buildings or Structures

This part of the insurance policy covers the structure of the building, as well as the mechanical equipment (HVAC, boilers, etc.). The policy that covers the structure also includes plumbing, electrical systems, gas, roofs, gutters, drains and downspouts, walls, and more. In other words, the structure part of the policy includes the building inside and out. If you rent or lease the building, then this part of your insurance policy covers damage to the inside of the building.

The structure section of the policy requires that the building be maintained properly, for it does not cover neglect or poor maintenance. Let's take the example of a roof leak. The insurance policy would pay for repairs if the leak came from a tree striking the roof or from shingles blown off in a hurricane or tornado. It would not cover a leak because the roof was not maintained properly or was long overdue for a new tarring. In addition, insurance may not pay if there was a leak and subsequent water damage, and the facilities and maintenance department did not cover the hole in the roof in a timely fashion. So if your building has a leak in the roof and the facilities and maintenance department knows about it but does not allocate funds or manpower to repair the leak, the institution would be responsible for any subsequent damage as a result of the leak. In other words, the institution did not mitigate the damage and therefore is responsible for any additional damage and costs.

As of 2002, no insurance policy covers mold damage or removal.[7] It is therefore essential that building envelopes and mechanical equipment be maintained properly, that all leaks and water damage be treated immediately, and that the source of water leaks or excess moisture be found and repaired with all due haste. Water damage and excess moisture from the air-handling system will most likely result in a mold infection.

Contents

This part of the insurance policy deals with the fixtures and furnishings of the library or archive. It includes desks, shelving, curtains, office equipment, and more. It does not cover the collection. The contents policy would cover loss of or damage to office equipment, although probably not computers, because they may fall under a separate part of the policy. (See the checklist "Insurance: Office Equipment" in appendix A.)

Electronic Data Processing (EDP)

Electronic data processing riders cover damage to computer equipment and, in some cases, the loss of stored data.[8] They also cover the restoration of computer operations at a remote site (hot site or cold site), the leasing of computer equipment, and associated technology. EDP riders are designed to cover expenses for two to three months. By that time, the computer operations department should either be back at its home or in an alternative long-term site. (See the checklist "Insurance: Computer Hardware" in appendix A.)

Collections: Special Papers Riders

Insurance policies have a variety of riders. One of them is "special papers," which includes the books, manuscripts, and audiovisual materials in libraries, archives, historical societies, and museums. There will be minimum and maximum amounts of coverage for loss of or damage to collections. You should have some idea of the total worth of your collection, the total number of books, and other information of this type.

Most libraries with circulating collections insure the institution for the loss of one-third to one-half of the collections. If the collection doesn't circulate at all, you want a different rider; use the insurance formula for special collections and rare books that is discussed below. Up to one-third of the collection is generally out in circulation at any one time. So how do you figure the amount to insure the collection? Well, you could just take the approximate value of the collection as a whole and divide it into thirds. Another method would be to look at the average replacement costs for the various types of books in your collection, including the processing and cataloging costs, and use those numbers. Today, fiction books range from $25 to $35 per title, including processing, cataloging, and staff time. Nonfiction books range from $50 to $75 per title (including processing costs); and reference materials, especially encyclopedias and multivolume works, start at $300 and could cost as much as $10,000 or more to replace. Regarding audiovisual materials, videos start at $20, DVDs start at $30 for single discs, and CDs average $20 per disc, with series costing more. Microforms can cost more than $100 per roll to replace, depending on the type of microform, the publisher, and the size of the microform publication.

Archives: Valuable Papers and Records Riders

In addition to printed book collections and audiovisual materials, your collection may contain archives, pamphlets, and manuscripts. Valuable papers and records riders also cover business records, documents, and other materials that identify and represent the institution as a legal entity. Insuring these items is much more difficult. Without some type of estimate of the value and purchasing costs for this part of your collection, it is more difficult to assign monetary value to these items. (See the checklist "Insurance: Archives" in appendix A.)

The nature of archives is to hold unique items and collections of materials, be they records of the institution, an organization, or an individual. Once destroyed, the items are gone, unless the materials were microfilmed or digitized. Microfilm and digital formats are great for use copies, but they may not be sufficient for researchers. Nevertheless, conversion to another format prevents loss of the intellectual content just as reprints of out-of-print books do. For collections of the institution's vital records (business records and legal documents), surrogates should be made and the originals stored where they cannot be damaged, in either remote storage facilities or off-site repositories.

So how do you insure the manuscripts in the collection? You should keep records of the price paid for collections purchased or the values assigned when collections are acquired from a donor. If funding was provided with the donation, this is a starting point for assigning value. Another method of determining the value of manuscript collections is to have them appraised for monetary value, that is, what it would cost to purchase the collections in today's market. It is not easy to find an appraiser for archival materials and records. You can find a list of appraisers at the Society of American Archivists website, http://www.archivists.org/saagroups/acq-app/appraisers.asp, or talk to your insurance company.

Special and Rare Collections

Separate insurance riders can be purchased for rare book collections and special collections that cover the average cost or value of the books in today's market. Items above a certain value, say $10,000 or $100,000, should be itemized and appraised. Insurance coverage is then figured on the total number of books in the collection times the average replacement cost (approximately $250–$300 per volume), with the scheduled items being separately insured. A file containing the appraisal, along with photographs or documentation of ownership and provenance, should be stored off-site with the insurance policy. (See the checklist "Insurance: Special Collections and Rare Books" in appendix A.)

Artwork

Just as rare books, special collections, and archives materials are difficult if not impossible to place a value upon, so is art. However, if you want some type of remuneration for lost or damaged artwork, you must assign a value to it. You will want two types of insurance for your art, one for theft and one for individual pieces. The first covers a maximum agreed-upon amount for the theft or damage to artwork, but not any specific items. It may not cover all that was lost. The second type covers specific, named items, the same as the rare books rider, for those listed, usually at market value. (See the checklist "Insurance: Artwork" in appendix A.)

In order to insure your art collection, you need to inventory the items and have them appraised. Photograph and document each item that is inventoried. Update the appraisals no less than every five years. Do not forget to insure the art collection for sprinkler, water, and flood damage and for theft.[9] There are a number of insurance companies that cover artwork or have programs for cultural institutions. For a list of such companies, see appendix C.

Commercial Off-Site Storage

If your collections and electronic data are stored off-site in a commercial storage facility (i.e., a facility not owned by your institution), the insurance policy should cover the items for theft, mutilation, fire, and water damage. First check on the reputation of the company and ask for references. Ask if its employees are bonded and insured and if the company does national criminal background checks on new hires.

You want to determine if there has ever been a fire, flood, or theft at the facility and if so, what the outcome was. Ask what the storage facility's insurance coverage includes and then be certain that the rider you purchase adequately covers those items stored within the building. Ask the storage company about the environmental conditions in the warehouse, what their security entails, and the types of fire detection and suppression systems used. Tour the facility, with the disaster response team leader if possible, and look for signs of damage or environmental problems such as mold, standing water, or discolored storage boxes. Ask how they control access to the materials stored on their site.

Consider the types of materials you are storing off-site and their security requirements. Are you sending sensitive or restricted office records or personnel records? Who is authorized to retrieve what you request, and how quickly? Are you storing electronic data and backups of digital resources off-site? Are you storing the backup computer records for the institution or the catalog system? Again, you want to know who has access to the records while they are in storage and when they are requested for shipment back to your institution. You will want insurance for the materials both while they are in storage off-site and while they are transported to your institution.

Shipping and Transportation for Exhibition or Conservation

Insurance is essential when materials are scheduled for exhibition. All items should be insured from the time they leave the lending institution until they arrive home. If yours is the lending institution, you will want to purchase an additional insurance rider that protects your materials during shipping and/or transport. This rider is called *transit insurance*. Transit insurance covers the object while it is in transit from one location to the next. In some cases, signing the contract with the shipping company may alleviate the company of any financial responsibility for damage in transit, so read it carefully.

Specialized courier services work with museums and know how to transport, store, and handle valuable objects. Of course, these couriers should be bonded and insured against loss or damage. Check the references of these companies to determine how long they have been in business and what type of personnel they hire. Do they have long-term employees or frequent turnover? What types of background checks and training do they provide to their couriers? This is particularly important if they pack and ship materials. How much experience does the company and its employees have handling books, library collections, and artwork? Check to see if the company has had any claims filed against it, and if so, how they were resolved.

It goes without saying that the materials being shipped should be packaged so that they are not damaged in the normal course of transport and handling. Each item should be inventoried and its condition documented, especially if the item is not in perfect condition. Digital images or photographs, along with written descriptions of each item, should accompany the shipment. The same information should be forwarded to the borrowing institution and retained at the lending institution for insurance purposes.

Exhibition

Borrowing institutions should check with their insurance carriers to confirm that their valuable papers and documents rider is sufficient to cover loss or damage to any borrowed objects for the length of time they are stored and exhibited at another institution. The same is true of the lending institution. Part of the negotiation and agreement for the exhibition should include who carries the various types of insurance covering what materials or the potential risks that exist. You will want to get the terms of the insurance coverage, including limitations, in writing prior to packing and shipping the materials. While on loan, the objects should be covered from the time they enter the grounds of the borrowing institution until they leave. This insurance is traditionally carried by the borrowing institution, and it should cover any and all locations the materials will occupy, including storage areas, loading docks, and exhibit areas.

Conservation Treatment Off-Site

Just as you purchase an insurance rider for collections and art objects that are sent for exhibitions, you want insurance for materials sent for conservation treatment. Usually the conservation facility has insurance coverage for the materials on-site. You want to get coverage for packing and shipping or transport. Ask the conservation facility if their insurance coverage includes items stored in their on-site or off-site storage facilities. If it does not, then you will want the rider to cover storage while the materials are awaiting treatment.[10] This insurance rider should include coverage not only against theft and mutilation, but also against loss due to fire, water, and poor environmental conditions. Again, complete documentation, a visual image, and provenance are essential. The American Institute for Conservation of Historic and Artistic Works (http://aic.stanford.edu) has an excellent brochure on guidelines for selecting a conservator. Some commercial insurance carriers are listed in appendix C.

Notes

1. Susan Laiming and Paul Laiming, *Insurances for the Public Library* (Chicago: Illinois Library Trustee Association, 1986), 1–2.
2. Ibid.
3. Ibid., 2–3.
4. Ibid.
5. Ibid., 3.
6. The Rare Books and Manuscripts Section of the Association of College and Research Libraries has a brochure about evaluating "rare books," *Your Old Books* (Chicago: American Library Association, 2005), 8; available at http://www.rbms.info/yob.shtml.
7. The topic of mold is beyond the subject of this publication. There is more information about the insurance industry and mold at the website of the Insurance Information Institution, http://www.iii.org/media/research/mold/.
8. Karen Sherbine, "Closing the Book on Library Losses," *Best's Review: Property/Casualty* 92, no. 4 (August 1992): 64.
9. For a complete discussion of this topic, see the Ontario Ministry of Culture's Museum Insurance Note 5 in "Museum Notes," http://www.culture.gov.on.ca/english/heritage/museums/munote5.htm.
10. Sherbine, "Closing the Book," 68.

Part

3

SAFETY

Chapter 10

Patron and Staff Safety

Libraries, museums, and archives are seen as safe places to visit, use, and work in.[1] Unfortunately, there have been incidents in cultural institutions that resulted in injuries or kidnapping or that involved guns or bomb threats. The chapters that follow look at the safety of our users and employees. We want to encourage people to use and enjoy the vast resources in our cultural institutions' collections. Therefore, it is essential that we reinforce the impression that libraries and museums are safe places in which to work.

Parents leave their children and teenagers at libraries for long periods of time, assuming they are safe. It is certainly better than leaving them at home alone. Individuals who are homeless or live in shelters go to the library because it is warm or quiet and a safe place to hang out. Students and adults, researchers and faculty come to cultural institutions to explore the resources and intellectual riches within.

It is important to maintain the tradition of cultural institutions as safe havens and workplaces. To do this, we must consider how best to protect our users and staff by being conscious of who is in the building and how they are behaving.

The safety of the patrons and staff is essential. We have been examining the building inside and out to make certain users and staff can enter, use the facility, and exit without injury, whether leaving for the night or during an emergency. Now we need to think about keeping patrons and staff safe from one another.

CASE STUDY

Just as the library is closing for the weekend, the librarian in charge finds a child in the stacks engrossed in a book. The child comes to the library regularly and usually leaves before closing time, but not this night. The librarian tells the child it is time to leave and the child says he is waiting to be picked up. So the librarian tells the child that she will leave the door open so when his ride arrives he can exit the building. The child wanders away to wait in a reading area and the librarian, thinking the child has left already, locks up without telling the cleaning staff there is a child awaiting pickup. The next thing the child knows, the head of the cleaning staff is standing there telling him the building is closed. The child says he is waiting for his ride and is informed that the building is closed and locked to the public, and he will have to leave now. So the child leaves and goes to the house of friends without calling home first. The cleaning staff members have finished cleaning and gone home. Unbeknownst to the child, his parents have come to pick him up only to find the building locked. They call home to see if their child has returned. When the answer is no, the parents call the police to check the library for their child.

The police arrive to find the building locked and dark, and they seem to have no way to contact the librarian to come open up and check the building. A heated conversation ensues between the parents and the police as to the location of the child and the likelihood that this is routine behavior. Eventually the child arrives home and the issue appears to be resolved. The next day, the head librarian calls the parents to complain that the child remained at the library after closing, not having been picked up in a timely manner. The parents are unhappy because their child was sent home after dark and was not permitted to call to check on his ride. No adult waited with the child; he was sent out in the dark alone.

While this story seems implausible, it did occur, or at least these are the public details. It appears that there is fault on both sides. Let's look at what the child should have done first.

The child should have

- been more alert to closing time
- asked to use the phone and call home
- never left the circulation desk after realizing the library was closed
- either waited outside the door or gone directly home after being told to leave

The librarian in charge put the child's safety at risk. The librarian should have

- told the child to call home using the circulation desk phone
- made certain the child stayed at the circulation desk until his ride arrived
- never have "left the door unlocked" for the child's ride and gone home, but waited for the pickup
- told the cleaning staff about the child

The head of the cleaning staff should have

- had the child call home and then wait for his ride at the door

Whatever fault we assign to the staff and the child, there are risks associated with the actions in this case study. The first is the safety of the child. No child, or even an adult, should be left alone in a library. You never know when someone might have an accident and be so injured that he or she cannot call for help. There is additional risk to a child being left without adult supervision. Children may be injured or abused by their peers or an adult, or even kidnapped. Even adults should not be alone in the library after all regular staff members have gone home for the night. Patrons should be escorted out; security should be alerted if there are staff members working after hours.

Under no circumstances should the librarian in the case study have left the door unlocked after closing. The librarian risked both the physical safety of the child and herself, and the security of the collections from unauthorized after-hours removal or mutilation of materials.

Unattended children (or "latchkey children") of any age are most problematic, because they are left for long periods of time in the library without adult supervision.[2] Anything can happen to these children, and it is not technically the library's place to be responsible for their safety. This issue becomes serious when the library is closed due to a weather emergency or for safety reasons. Unattended children may not be able to reach their parents and may have no safe place to go during the day other than the library. The library should have some type of policy in place to call the police or social services to come and care for unattended children if the building closes early.

In our case study, the child should have called home and asked about his ride. The librarian should have made the child call and then wait up front, in plain sight, for his ride. For safety reasons, at no time should the child have been left in the building alone with the door unlocked. For that matter, there should always be two people in the library.

Establish safety policies to ensure that no one is left in the building when the library or archive is closed. Security staff should work their way through the building to ensure no one is left behind. Establish a policy for sending unattended children to a safe place, a police or fire station, or a social services agency. Make this policy known to all parents, staff members, and security personnel, as well as the neighborhood's public safety departments. In this way, someone will know what happened and where to find these unattended children.

PROBLEM BEHAVIOR

Establish and post policies that describe appropriate conduct and behavior in the building.[3] Behaviors and practices that are not acceptable should be clearly defined. You must enforce these policies uniformly, first with a warning and then with whatever restrictions or revocations of privileges are published in your policies.

Warnings to cease inappropriate behavior are often given first by senior staff, department heads, and administrators. All staff should be comfortable making such comments. If the patron does not abide by the policies after a warning, then contact your security department or department head if there are no security guards in your building. Depending on the policy and the size of the institution, the security department should give the next warning and then enforce the policy by escorting the patron out of the building and perhaps off the institution's grounds. The next step is to restrict that patron's access to the facility.

If the behavior results in harm to a patron or staff member, or damage to collections, hardware, software, or the facility itself, call the police. If the patron's actions are threatening toward other patrons or staff, notify security immediately and then the police. The policies should be enforced and charges pressed.

CHILDREN AND YOUNG ADULTS

It is not uncommon for there to be unattended children in the public library. They can be left alone during the day or through the evening while their parents are working. Keeping the children who use our collections safe is a concern. Establish policies that protect the children from harm and from strangers.[4]

Not only does the library have to be cognizant that there are unattended children in the facility, but there are instances when these children and others are noisy, disruptive, or abusive to other children. You can establish a policy that limits the number of children who can work at one table, or you can set aside a room for group or loud activity. If there are preteens and teenagers hanging out, set a limit as to their number. Some libraries have their security guards patrol the children's and young adult areas more frequently after school lets out and during the summer. Other libraries attempt to keep children out of the adult reading rooms and reference areas with varying success. This is especially difficult when the children and young adults are doing their homework using the adult reference collections. If the noise levels become intolerable, then ask the security guards or a supervisor to warn the children to be quiet or leave. If the children, teens, and preteens are being rowdy, disruptive, or abusive, remind them that they are in a library and should be reading or studying, or they have to leave. Be certain to have policies posted and enforced evenly, and reinforced when noise levels get out of control.

In addition to trying to control children and young adults, the librarians and other staff members should be aware of what else is happening in their part of the library. If there are unattended children in the room, then the staff should be alert to adults without children. Do the adults appear to be looking for materials, or are they looking at the children? Watch to see if they follow the children to the restrooms or the hall outside them. If you think there is something suspicious going on, call security and have them confront the adult. If you see a parent abusing or hitting a child, remind the parent that hitting is prohibited in the library. If the parent persists, call a supervisor, a security guard, or the police. Do not touch the parent or get between the parent and the child. Document the incident and follow the library's policy regarding disruptive, abusive, or belligerent behavior.

ADULT PATRONS

The nature of libraries, archives, museums, and historical societies is to attract people to come inside to use and peruse the resources available. Unless your institution is a private organization, it cannot limit who enters the building and uses the collections. So you may have homeless, mentally impaired, or itinerant users amid the usual businesspeople, students, and other residents of your community.

There are a number of books that describe how to handle problem patrons.[5] They describe the personalities of problem patrons who range from malodorous to belligerent and offensive. Both Bruce Shuman and Anne Turner cover the topic with case studies and recommended solutions, as well as sample policies. They emphasize that problem patrons have the right to use the library and ask staff for assistance, but not the right to abuse these privileges. The library staff, supported by its administration, must support these limits.

It is a realistic expectation of patrons and staff that the library be clean, the restrooms be safe, and the stacks be for browsing materials. Patrons and staff should never have to worry about their safety in the stacks. If a staff member encounters unacceptable behavior, then she should tell the patron in a calm, nonthreatening manner that his behavior is inappropriate and ask him to stop. If this behavior continues, then call security. Inappropriate behavior includes sexual exposure and behavior, roughhousing, loud or raucous conversations that disturb other patrons, running, and fighting. Patrons who habitually sleep in the library should be asked to wake up and leave.

For your own safety, never touch a patron if he is sleeping, because you do not know how he will react. In fact, you should never touch a patron at all, because you do not want to be accused of abuse or assault.

There is other behavior that may disturb or unsettle reference and circulation staff. This behavior might include patrons who ask questions of a sexual nature or questions that are personal. Answer in a calm manner that these questions are inappropriate and ask the patron to stop. If this does not work, call a supervisor to deal with the patron. If the staff member is alone in that department, contact a senior staff member or a supervisor in the building or call security.

UNCOMFORTABLE OR SUSPICIOUS REFERENCE QUESTIONS

Since September 11, 2001, we have become more conscious of unusual reference questions. These questions might include addresses for and pictures of public officials, maps and drawings of public and government buildings, or designs for bombs and weapons. Just remember, sometimes these questions are part of a homework assignment.

Within days of September 11, 2001, a staff member in a map room was asked for building drawings and layouts for the government buildings in their downtown. The staff member was very uncomfortable with the request. Most of the facility's users were regulars, but this patron was unknown and obviously unfamiliar with that type of research. The department had no plan in place to deal with such a question and the staff member panicked, fumbling to try to provide the information without asking for details or calling for a colleague to help out. A better course of action would have been for the staff member to call the back office or a supervisor and ask that they come to assist with a difficult question. In the course of discussing the question, away from the patron, they could have alerted security. With a more complete reference interview, it is possible the staff member would have found that the request was quite innocent.

What should you do if this happens to you? If you are at all uncomfortable answering a reference question, pick up the phone to consult a supervisor. Tell the patron that you must consult with the appropriate department to obtain that information. Try to stall the patron until you can get assistance or clarify the purpose of her question.

Establish an emergency phrase that alerts staff and security to call for additional assistance or to call the police. There should be a silent alarm or panic button that rings in either the security department or the police department in the event of an emergency or disturbance. Test it to see the speed and type of response.

DIFFICULT PATRONS

People with every imaginable personality type use the library: patrons who ask odd questions just to talk to someone because they are lonely; patrons who argue with staff about policy; patrons who argue with other patrons; and those who just hang around because they do not have anywhere else to go. Libraries and archives (and historical societies and museums to a lesser extent, because they usually charge an admission fee) are safe, warm, comfortable places for the homeless, for people who are mentally ill, and for patrons who are annoying, unpleasant, obnoxious, or loud; use obscene language; have unpleasant body odor; or sleep or sit at computers all day and surf the Internet. As long as these patrons are not bothering anyone, you cannot ban them from the library. However, Turner talks about librarians and security staff who have required malodorous patrons to return after bathing and washing their clothes.[6]

The more problematic patrons are those who hide in the stacks and make inappropriate sexual advances toward patrons and staff members. If and when you encounter patrons who are acting this way, inform the patron that this is inappropriate behavior, ask him to stop, and if he persists, call the security guards. Staff members who shelve books are the most vulnerable to sexual advances, as are reference staff members who take patrons into the stacks to help them find the materials they seek. Installing convex mirrors to show out-of-sight stacks areas is one way to cut down on inappropriate behavior and protect staff members from harm. Establish written policies that prohibit inappropriate sexual behaviors in the library and post them with the other policies.

AGGRESSIVE PATRONS

There are many reasons for patrons to seem aggressive. They may be frustrated by their research project or by the responses to questions posed to staff members, or they may be troubled or mentally ill. Sometimes patrons are large or tall and so seem to be aggressive when they are just in your personal space. This is especially true if staff members are sitting at an information desk. These patrons are not necessarily aggressive; they are merely overwhelming. You can lessen this sensation of aggression by standing up and moving away slightly, adjusting your personal space.

Once in a while, there is a patron who is aggressive or upset when arriving at the reference or information desk. Listen carefully to the complaint or problem, rephrase the comment, and try to answer it without upsetting him more. Try to defuse the situation by getting the patron to explain what is wrong or why he is so upset. It is possible that he is phrasing his questions using different or unfamiliar terminology. Perhaps he cannot articulate the problem or is having trouble expressing himself clearly. Take a little extra time to listen, and that attention should calm him down. Active listening is a technique that involves reiterating what the patron asks using synonyms. This requires some practice, because it can seem patronizing. Get the patron to describe what he wants to do with the information or what the end purpose of the research is. Together you can puzzle out what he is seeking. It may be that your institution uses a different jargon than the one he usually works with. From the other side of the desk, the patron is being persistent because he knows or assumes that the information is there. Shifting perspective and "thinking outside the box" are keys to alleviating this form of aggression.

Let's move on to the verbally abusive patron. These are patrons who are manifesting abusive or inappropriate language and can be quite agitated. Again, try to calm the patron down by listening carefully. Try not to assume a defensive or aggressive posture. Whatever you do, don't touch the patron. This could result in a physical response. If the aggressive or abrasive behavior escalates, ask another staff member or a supervisor to assist the patron. If you think the patron is going to hit you, call security. Beware of shuffling the patron off to a staff member who cannot make a decision or help him. This is particularly true when the patron is upset about his overdue fines or missing books. Give circulation staff members enough authority to waive fines if this action will defuse the situation. Establish guidelines and criteria for waiving fines, and for asking the supervisor to take over. When in doubt, ask a supervisor to take charge. If the patron becomes physically aggressive, calmly call security. Do not turn your back on the patron. When in doubt, ask for help.

Take some time to discuss procedures with the staff for working with aggressive patrons and defusing difficult situations. Work with your security department and community public safety departments to learn techniques to calm down irate patrons and passively protect your staff members.

You can devise code words for staff to use to alert others when there is a problem with a patron or a situation. Work with staff so they understand when and how to use the code words. Emphasize that their safety and the safety of the patrons come first.

Sometimes it is better to use the code words for help or to push the panic button at the reference or circulation desk than to handle an irate patron alone. It is essential that staff members alert security guards, back room staff, administrators, or police if they think they are in danger. In turn, administrators must support the staff member's or supervisor's decision, and if there is reason to prosecute the offender, do so.

These are not the only troublesome patrons in your library. You will find patrons who ask questions just to ask them, ones who ask incessant questions, and those who just ask strange questions. Turner has some wonderful suggestions for working with these particular patrons. Staff members need to be creative, consistent, and patient when dealing with patrons. It's part of the job.

INTRUDERS, BOMB THREATS, HOSTAGE THREATS, AND GUNMEN

It is a sad but true fact that libraries and archives, historical societies, and museums have been the location of gunfire and bomb threats. Let's deal with these problems one at a time.

If you or anyone on your staff receives a bomb threat, ask the informant to tell you when the bomb is going to go off, what type of bomb it is, where it is, and other questions that show your interest. Try to maintain a calm voice and attitude. While on the phone, pass a note to the nearest staff member to call the police or security immediately. Do not do this yourself or put the caller on hold! Talk to the caller and get him to tell all. If danger seems imminent or when the security department instructs you to, evacuate the building and gather in a remote location well away from the building. This safe location should be the same place as in your disaster response plan. Do not reenter the building until the fire department or the bomb squad authorizes it.

As discussed earlier, in chapter 2, signs should be posted prohibiting weapons of all types, including concealed weapons, in the building. You can list them if you wish, and they should include all types of firearms and knives of all shapes and sizes. If there is gunfire in the building, evacuate the building as carefully as possible, sending patrons either outside or to the tornado shelters. Call the police immediately upon exiting the building or area. If there is gunfire in your immediate vicinity, get onto the floor behind furniture or some other type of solid protection, if possible. Do not move until the area is secured by the security department or by police or fire officers.

Have the security or police department talk to your staff about how to handle threats. It is possible they will perform a safety audit for your buildings. If not, there are a number of consulting firms that do this for a fee. Follow their suggestions when designing and implementing security and safety policies.

EMERGENCY EVACUATION DRILLS: FIRE, TORNADOES, AND BAD WEATHER

The staff and the patrons must leave the building immediately when the fire alarm rings. Gather the staff at the outside location as identified by the disaster response team or by the security planning team. This gathering place should be well outside the building and easily accessible. There should be a secondary site far from the building or even outside the institution where staff can gather if the campus is inaccessible. If possible, select a location that is sheltered from the weather. Do not reenter the building until you are told to do so.

If you hear the air raid sirens, they usually indicate a tornado sighting. In some communities, they indicate bad storms or hurricanes. Direct your patrons to the underground tornado shelters or to a place within the building that has no windows. Do not leave this shelter until the all-clear siren is sounded or you are instructed to do so by security or public safety officers.

Some institutions use floor or department safety wardens to direct patrons and staff to the appropriate emergency exit or shelter. At some time prior to a disaster or bad-weather alert, discuss how to help wheelchair-bound patrons to a safe location. Talk with your security department and fire department about this matter so they are aware of where handicapped patrons and staff might be in the event of a disaster, fire, or emergency.

COORDINATING RESPONSES TO EMERGENCIES

The procedures and policies described above also pertain to your disaster response plan. Coordinate your actions with the security and safety division of your institution and with the disaster response team. Design procedures for responding to various types of emergencies. (See the checklist "Emergency Response Procedures" in appendix A.) This is doubly important if there is no formal disaster response plan at your library's parent institution. The priorities of the institution may not correspond with those of the library. The institution may focus on the infrastructure and on students or patrons. You are concerned about the collections and valuable resources housed within the buildings. Indeed, the library or archive may be a very low priority in the institution's recovery plan. Create your plan, send it to the institution's committee, and then proceed with making it as efficient as possible to get the collections accessible and functioning as quickly as possible. It might be helpful to consult various books on disaster response planning while creating this part of your security plan.

STAFF

There is a wide range of opinions about protecting the safety of staff from patrons and from other staff; that is, interpersonal relations. Shuman and Turner both cover these issues in their publications. Human resources departments usually have policies and procedures for dealing with interpersonal relations issues. So we will take a brief look at the issue of protecting staff.

Common sense prevails when we look at the safety of staff. No one should ever work in the building by themselves. This happens sometimes when a staff member works while the building is closed. The security guard (or someone else if you don't have a guard) must know when that person enters and leaves the building.

Try to establish a security policy that protects the physical safety of the staff member, requiring that she notify someone or receive permission ahead of time to be in the building alone. This is particularly important if the building is cleaned and serviced after everyone goes home for the day. Not being alone in the building seems like common sense, but remember the number of times this has occurred because of scheduling and vacation conflicts or unexpected illness on the weekends.

There should never be just one person staffing the building and working with the public. We know this occurs because of drastically reduced staffing or because it is the weekend. Nevertheless, this is not the best of situations for a variety of reasons. Accidents happen and staff members get sick, or there could be an emergency. Work schedules should include an alternate or on-call staff member who can fill in when someone calls in sick. Holidays, nights, and weekends are common times when staffing is minimal. These are times when there is only one professional staff member or, in the case of colleges and universities, when there are only student workers at public service desks. The same may be true in smaller historical societies when there are only volunteers working. As a rule of thumb, never schedule fewer than two staff members in the building and serving the public at any one time. In addition, there should always be some senior staff member on call during the hours the facility is open, to answer questions and respond to an emergency at the library or archive.

At these times a senior staff member, administrator, or supervisor should be on call and available by phone should a problem arise. No matter what, on every shift, someone should be designated who is authorized to make a decision. These decisions include but are not limited to evacuating the building in case of an emergency, sending people to an emergency shelter or safe zone in case of bad weather or a tornado, and calling security guards and the police to deal with a crisis or a problem patron. If such a problem arises, the on-call senior staff member or administrator should be notified. The decisions made by the student, volunteer, or junior staff member when faced with the emergency or threat to the safety of the staff and patrons should not be countermanded or denigrated. Decisions were made when the crisis occurred. It is the responsibility of the senior staff and administrators to support those decisions. This being the case, it is important that whoever is the designated supervisor for a shift knows the institution's policies and has the ability to make informed decisions.

Another factor to consider is the staff's perception of their own safety while in the building. Not only should they feel safe during the day while at reference, information, and circulation desks, but while in their offices and workrooms. Many institutions require their staff to wear name tags or badges for identification. These badges permit access to nonpublic areas of the building. Volunteers, visitors, and workmen should receive visitor badges. With this requirement, staff can easily identify one another and know when unauthorized persons enter nonpublic areas. The beauty of identification badges is that they can be key cards and can be programmed to prohibit access to restricted areas such as special collections and rare book rooms, storage areas, and rare book vaults. Computer programs at security stations monitor and record which key cards are used where and when. If the information is kept for long enough, it might enable security to identify thefts and unauthorized intrusions.

It is important for staff members to feel that the library or archive is safe if they routinely work in their offices and workrooms after hours, at night, and over the weekend. Working when the building is closed is more common at academic institutions. Staff members working in libraries, archives, historical societies, and museums tend to focus on administrative tasks when the building is closed to the public. Security guards should be present during all hours that staff work in the building, and particularly when staff members routinely work when the building is closed to the public. By the way, this is also a time when conferences and consultations are scheduled, because these activities do not interfere with public service responsibilities. So it is even more important to keep track of visitors when there are meetings on closed days.

Establish security and safety policies for staff members who work after hours so they know whom to call in an emergency, whether it is security guards, supervisors, or the police. Post phone numbers by office phones for easy access.

OTHER EMPLOYEES

As we discussed earlier, the security department should run a background check on all cleaning staff and maintenance staff as well as on security guards. If the institution hires a company to do these jobs, then the security department should run a background check on the company and make certain it is bonded and insured. Security guards must be on duty at all times when there are contractors or cleaning and maintenance staff in the building. Again, this is to protect the safety of these employees and contactors and to protect the collections from theft and mutilation.

Notes

1. For visitors' perceptions of safety, see the comment in Bonnie Pitman, "Muses, Museums, and Memories," in "America's Museums," special issue, *Daedalus* 128, no. 3 (Summer 1999): 16.
2. Anne M. Turner, "'It's Free and It's Safe': Handling Problems with Unattended Children," in *It Comes with the Territory: Handling Problem Situations in Libraries,* rev. ed. (Jefferson, NC: McFarland, 2004), 68–70, 150–51.
3. For guidelines for writing policies for libraries, see Sandra Nelson and June Garcia, *Creating Policies for Results: From Chaos to Clarity* (Chicago: American Library Association, 2003). For examples of policies, see Turner, *It Comes with the Territory,* appendix 3.
4. The State Library of Ohio has a number of sample policies on its website, including "Rules of Behavior in Library Facilities" and "Unattended Children"; see http://winslo.state.oh.us/publib/policies.html. See also the policies of the Columbus (Ohio) Metropolitan Library in its "Customer Code of Conduct" section, http://www.columbuslibrary.org/ebranch/index.cfm?pageid=88.
5. See the recommendations and policies in Bruce A. Shuman, *Library Security and Safety Handbook: Prevention, Policies, and Procedures* (Chicago: American Library Association, 1999); and in Turner, *It Comes with the Territory.*
6. Turner, *It Comes with the Territory,* 26–27.

Chapter 11

Security and Safety Departments

Security and safety departments have a wide range of responsibilities within any institution, and are called upon to cope with emergencies ranging from problematic or violent patrons to fires and bomb threats. Many security guards are off-duty or retired law enforcement officers from police and fire departments. Others were members of the armed forces, holding positions within the military police. Even if your entire security staff does not have professional training, the head of the department should. Smaller institutions may dispense with security staff and instead depend on the local public safety departments, including local fire and police, for protection during an emergency.

Ideally, members of the security department should be given professional training. The hiring institution should run national background checks on all security guards and check their references prior to hiring. Nonprofessional security guards (i.e., those who do not come from law enforcement or the military) should be trained in self-defense, know when to use their weapons, and know how to defuse a potentially violent situation without injuring innocent bystanders. In earlier chapters we discussed the need to screen individuals for weapons upon entering the facility. If nothing else, this prescreening prevents potentially violent situations.

Smaller institutions and public libraries may have security guards with no professional training who confirm that books were checked out. When they are called upon to handle unruly and disruptive patrons or potentially violent situations, they ask for assistance from the public safety community. This forces the institution to establish an excellent working relationship with local fire, police, and emergency medical response departments. In turn, you can ask these public safety departments to provide appropriate education for your nonprofessional security staff members. No matter what their training, all the security guards should be physically capable of handling their jobs and escorting patrons from the building.

Large institutions usually have a public safety office or security office whose personnel are responsible for safety and security throughout the entire campus or institution. They deal with issues as diverse as fire protection; policing buildings and grounds, parking areas, and vehicular traffic; and protecting students, staff, and visitors twenty-four hours a day. Some libraries and archives have separate staff to monitor their building and check everyone who enters and exits. Other security guards perform regular surveillance and walk-through inspections. The responsibilities of security and safety personnel in museums and historical societies are as diverse as those in libraries and archives.

Establish an active liaison relationship with this department for the security of collections. Ask for the same liaison as is assigned to the disaster response team. Assign a staff member to serve as liaison to the security department. Have an open discussion with security department staff in order to define their role within the safety plan. What is their responsibility vis-à-vis the library or archive? Discuss how they will maintain a physical presence in the library or archive while the building is open. How does their routine differ after hours? You may want to coordinate this meeting with a planning session of the disaster response team. Discuss appropriate emergency notification procedures for the library to contact security guards and vice versa.

Ask the security or safety department to describe its procedures for responding to crises. Ask for a copy of these procedures and incorporate them into your plan. It may be that the institution as a whole has already embarked upon a "continuous operations" plan or a contingency plan that outlines how the institution will function during an institutional or area-wide emergency. Discuss where the library or archive fits within the priorities of the institutional security plan. In turn, make the security department and the institution aware of your plans (security and disaster response) and the needs of the library or archive.

Another meeting with security might include a discussion about emergency exits, fire and smoke alarms, and security systems. Discuss how quickly security or safety personnel can respond after an alarm sounds. Depending on what type of alarm sounds, the appropriate security or safety personnel should respond immediately. You can set up tests and drills with the library and security staff to streamline notification and response procedures.

Also discuss other types of alarms and emergency notification systems, such as water alarms and panic buttons, with the security and safety department. Describe various situations and create response protocols and procedures for dealing with theft and disruptive behavior.

Find out how the security and safety department makes its guards visible to staff and patrons during their irregular patrols of public areas. Work with security and safety staff so that they are alert to mutilation of materials, theft, violence, and obscene or inappropriate behavior. Set up a training schedule for staff so the security guards or police can teach staff members to be vigilant in their observations of patrons' actions. Discuss how security guards monitor entrances to staff areas while being vigilant to patrons entering nonpublic areas. They can do this by either walking by on an irregular basis or by monitoring the entrances using cameras and key cards. Security should report and respond immediately to any unauthorized entrance. Security should carefully monitor the movement of construction contractors and temporary workers, contract maintenance personnel, and cleaning crews.

Other places to watch and secure against unauthorized entrance are emergency exits; doorways between staff and public areas, storage areas, and mechanical and service areas; and telecommunications, server, and utility closets. Separate keys or key cards should be used to gain entrance to these secure areas. The facilities and maintenance department should supervise any contractors who enter these parts of the building. They should never be given a key and told to just "go there and work on it." Someone should oversee their work and escort them out at the completion of the project. For the same reasons, no one should be left unsupervised in the telecommunications and network server rooms. Contractors and repair persons should be supervised by members of the IT or security department at all times. Security cameras should be positioned so they can monitor staff and contractor actions in these staff and maintenance areas.

The security or safety department should be notified of any employees or contractors who might be working in secure or nonpublic areas, especially after hours. Establish a policy that provides a list of contractors who will be working in the building. If you have a construction project going on in the building, ask if these contractors can have a different "visitors" badge to differentiate them from volunteer workers or the public. Talk to the security department to learn if there are background or security checks the institution runs before hiring contractors. How is the security department involved in the process?

Most of all, the administration must establish written policies to enforce the safety and security of the collections and users so there is a clear understanding of what are acceptable behavior and appropriate responses. Administrators must be willing to prosecute offenders, to the full extent of the law, for trespassing and for theft or mutilation of materials.

COMMUNITY PUBLIC SAFETY AGENCIES

Establish a relationship with the local fire and police departments. Use the same staff member who serves as your liaison to the security department at your institution. Other people to invite to a meeting might be the head of the library or archive, the security team, the disaster response team members, the facilities or maintenance manager, and the head of security and safety at your institution.

Hold a working meeting with fire and police department representatives while you are developing your plan and procedures. Take them on a tour of the public and staff areas as well as the emergency exits in the library or archive. Acquaint the fire department with the maintenance staff and the mechanical rooms so they are aware of where the shutoffs are located and any potential fire hazards within the building. Ask them to point out their security concerns and to suggest procedures for dealing with internal safety for people and security for collections and equipment.

Invite the fire marshal into your facility to discuss safety issues and to point out potential hazards and remedies. Include the head of your disaster response team in these discussions so you can both work on preventing crises.

State, county, and local emergency management agencies exist in your community and are establishing emergency response procedures and plans for dealing with community-wide incidents and crises. Set up a meeting with these officials or attend some of their meetings to learn where your parent institution, library, archive, historical society, or museum fits within their recovery schedules. Discuss how you can work together to protect your collections, equipment, and properties, and of course the people within the buildings.

During your meetings with the public safety community, help them understand the importance of the library or archive as a data and information resource center and a "safe" meeting place. Ask them to consider the library or archive for their emergency command post or meeting place. After all, it is heavily wired for telecommunications and Internet access, usually has a tornado shelter, and can be stocked with potable water and food.

Teach the public safety community about your safety and security plans as well as your disaster response plan. Emphasize your institution's ability to work independently from emergency management agencies to restore operations and deal with incidents should there be an area-wide emergency.

Appendix

A

Checklists

EMERGENCY RESPONSE PROCEDURES

Name of campus / building / department ______________________________

Potential Risk	Planned Actions or Responses	Person in Charge	Emergency Contact Number
Fire			
Water			
Theft			
Injury			
Damage to building			
Damage to doors or windows			
Computer problem or virus			
Power outage			
Phone outage			
Security alarm outage			
Security alarm activated			
Other accidents outside building			
Weather incidents:			
Tornado			
Hurricane			
Earthquake			
Blizzard			
Flood			
Wind damage			
Hail damage			
Other			

GENERAL COLLECTIONS: ENTRANCES

Yes No NA

❒ ❒ ❒ Are signs posted that prohibit concealed weapons?

❒ ❒ ❒ Are signs posted that indicate that belongings may be searched upon entering building or area?

❒ ❒ ❒ Is a list of permitted items posted at entrances?

❒ ❒ ❒ Are patrons required to show picture ID?

❒ ❒ ❒ Do security guards check for bound items?

❒ ❒ ❒ Do security guards check for electronic devices, register them, and match them with patron's ID?

❒ ❒ ❒ Are patrons and their belongings scanned for metal objects (concealed firearms, knives, etc.)?

❒ ❒ ❒ Are patrons directed to locker areas?

GENERAL COLLECTIONS: EXITS

What type of security is at patron exit to prevent materials from leaving without being checked out?

❒ Security gates and alarms

❒ Security guards

❒ Circulation desk

❒ No security

Do guards check inside bags and packages when patrons exit the building? ❒ Yes ❒ No ❒ NA

Do guards check all bound materials to see if they are property of the library? ❒ Yes ❒ No ❒ NA

Do guards check all electronic devices to confirm they belong to the patron and were brought into the building? ❒ Yes ❒ No ❒ NA

What actions do guards take when alarms sound at patrons' exit? ______________________________

____

What actions do staff take when alarms sound at patrons' exit? ______________________________

____

GENERAL COLLECTIONS: SECURITY OF THE COLLECTION

Print Materials

- ❒ Property stamps
- ❒ Security tags, Tattle-Tape, or stickers in books

Microfilm

- ❒ Property stamps on film boxes

Music Scores, Bound Pamphlets, Other Small or Thin Materials

- ❒ Property stamps on all parts
- ❒ Security devices or magnetized bar codes

Vertical Files or Pamphlet Materials

- ❒ Property stamps on items
- ❒ Bar codes or security devices on items
- ❒ Secure method for circulating items (large envelopes, see-through envelopes)
- ❒ Some method to track these items from circulation to return desk so that they are returned to the proper departments

Audiovisual Materials

- ❒ Property stamps on cases
- ❒ Property stamps or ID written in indelible ink on face of cassettes and videos, or on hub ring of CDs and DVDs
- ❒ Security tags or magnetized bar codes on face of cassettes, videos, CDs, and DVDs
- ❒ Security devices in cases for audiovisual materials
- ❒ High-theft items behind circulation desk

Books or Other Bound Materials with CDs or DVDs Attached

- ❒ Property markings on all materials
- ❒ Security devices on all materials
- ❒ Indication in record and on cover that more than one object is part of whole book

PROTECTING SPECIAL COLLECTIONS, RARE BOOKS, AND ARCHIVES

On-Site

Are the collections kept in a separate area of the building? ❒ Yes ❒ No ❒ NA

Are there security cameras? ❒ Yes ❒ No ❒ NA

How are entrances and exits controlled? ❒ Buzzer ❒ Key card ❒ Keypad ❒ Code

Are codes changed monthly? ❒ Yes ❒ No ❒ NA

Are codes changed when staff leave the department? ❒ Yes ❒ No ❒ NA

If department is on a separate floor, can elevator and stairwells be locked when department is closed? ❒ Yes ❒ No ❒ NA

Are there doors in the staff area to the rest of the building or collections? ❒ Yes ❒ No ❒ NA

If so, how is access limited? ❒ Security alarm ❒ Buzzer ❒ Key card ❒ Keypad ❒ Code

Is there a vault or locked room for items with high monetary value? ❒ Yes ❒ No ❒ NA

What are the hours the department is open? ______________________

What are the hours for cleaning staff access? ______________________

How frequently do security guards patrol reading room? when open __________ when closed __________

How frequently do security guards patrol stacks area? when open __________ when closed __________

Is this special collections area ever used for special events? ❒ Yes ❒ No ❒ NA

If so, how is security different on those occasions? ______________________

____

How is access to stacks areas restricted? ______________________

____

Are special collections, rare books, or archives on exhibit?

❒ Inside the reading room

❒ Outside the reading room but in the same basic area

❒ In the same building

❒ In other parts of the institution

❒ For loan and external (off institutional grounds) exhibition

❒ No exhibits

How are the collections secured from theft or damage while on display? ______________________

____

Off-Site Storage

Is there an off-site area for storage of special collections, rare books, or archives that are seldom used?
❒ Yes ❒ No ❒ NA

If so, are special collections intermingled with general collections' off-site storage? ❒ Yes ❒ No ❒ NA

Does security patrol the off-site storage? ❒ Yes ❒ No ❒ NA

Are there alarm and security systems in places off-site? ❒ Yes ❒ No ❒ NA

How is access to the items stored off-site restricted? ______________________

DEPARTMENT SURVEY: SPECIAL COLLECTIONS

Is there an emergency exit from this collection's reading room? ❐ Yes ❐ No ❐ NA

If yes, where is it located? ______________________________

If no, where is the nearest exit? ______________________________

Is there an emergency exit from the stacks area for this collection? ❐ Yes ❐ No ❐ NA

If yes, where is it located? ______________________________

If no, where is the nearest exit? ______________________________

Where do the alarms ring if the emergency door is used? ______________________________

Is there a security alarm or panic button in the special collections area reading room? ❐ Yes ❐ No ❐ NA

If so, who answers the alarm and how quickly? ______________________________

Is there a security alarm or panic button in the special collections stacks area? ❐ Yes ❐ No ❐ NA

If so, who answers the alarm and how quickly? ______________________________

Is there a phone in the special collections stacks area to facilitate contact with administration, security, or other departments in an emergency? ❐ Yes ❐ No ❐ NA

If so, does the phone in the reading room light up if this phone is used? ❐ Yes ❐ No ❐ NA

Mark the following on your floor plan for each special collections area:

❐ Windows

❐ Public entrance into special collections

❐ Doors between reading area and stacks area

❐ Doors between stacks area and rest of building or collections

❐ Break room or kitchen

❐ Staff offices

❐ Restrooms for public

❐ Restrooms for staff

❐ Emergency exits in staff area

Are there lockers or a secure area for patrons' belongings?

❐ Inside reading room

❐ Outside reading room

❐ No lockers

Are there lockers or a secure area for staff members' belongings? ❐ Yes ❐ No ❐ NA

If so, where it is located? ______________________________

SPECIAL COLLECTIONS: USE OF THE COLLECTION

Rare Books

Before giving requested item to patron

- ❒ Check for completeness
- ❒ Check for property marks and institutional identification
- ❒ Check that all plates and illustrative materials are present and note any that are missing
- ❒ Check for ephemera and slip-sheets within bound volumes
- ❒ Make a note of any damage, stray marks, etc.

Before placing returned items on cart for shelving

- ❒ Check for completeness
- ❒ Check that all plates and illustrative materials are present
- ❒ Check that all ephemera are present
- ❒ Look for any new damage, stray marks, etc.
- ❒ If any damage to item is noted either when bound item is given to patron or when it is returned and the item is not already stabilized (boxed), bring to attention of conservator or preservation officer.

Archives

Before giving requested box to patron

Is there an inventory with the collection or box? ❒ Yes ❒ No ❒ NA

Boxed materials are contained in ❒ file folders ❒ envelopes ❒ NA

Are folders or envelopes filed in a particular order? ❒ Yes ❒ No ❒ NA

Are folders or envelopes labeled with contents on outside? ❒ Yes ❒ No ❒ NA

Do items in folders or envelopes match labels? ❒ Yes ❒ No ❒ NA

Are items within folders in any order? ❒ Yes ❒ No ❒ NA

Are items marked with property stamps? ❒ Yes ❒ No ❒ NA

Before placing returned box on cart for shelving

Are all materials present and accounted for? ❒ Yes ❒ No ❒ NA

Are any items damaged? ❒ Yes ❒ No ❒ NA

If so, when was folder, box, or item given to patron? ______________ When was it returned? ______________

If an item requires treatment, has conservator or preservation officer been notified? ❒ Yes ❒ No ❒ NA

PATRON USING COLLECTIONS

Record patron's name, institution, address, phone number, and e-mail address

Attach a copy of the patron's picture ID to the application

Attach copies of any required credentials or letters of intent of research to the application

Record date of use

Record purpose of use of that part of collection

Record items requested

Record name of staff member on reference duty

Have patron sign and date collection use and rules policy

Check materials before giving them to patron for completeness, condition, and order

Give patron one folder or small collection at a time

Remind patron to replace items in their original order

Check materials after patron returns them for completeness, condition, and order

STORAGE AREAS

On Campus or in Building

Who has access? ___

How is the collection accessed? ___

Are there specific hours during which the storage area is accessible? ___

Is there a reading room for patrons? ❐ Yes ❐ No

Are there security cameras or motion detectors in the storage area? ❐ Yes ❐ No

How many doors give access to the storage area? ___

How are entrances secured? ___

Is there an alarm system or security on entrances and exits? ❐ Yes ❐ No

How often does security patrol the storage area? ___

When does the facilities and maintenance department clean inside the storage area? ___

When does the buildings and grounds department clean outside the facility? ___

If the storage area is below ground level, how often does someone check for unauthorized entrance or water damage? ___

Remote Storage Facility (Off-Site but Controlled by Institution or Consortium)

Which individuals, departments, and institutions have access to the remote storage facility? ___

___

How is the collection accessed at the remote storage facility? ___

How are materials sent to the remote storage facility? ___

How are materials in the remote storage facility transferred from one location to another? ❐ Employees ❐ Contractors

Are the contractors bonded and insured? ❐ Yes ❐ No

Did you perform a national criminal background and financial check on the contractors' company? ❐ Yes ❐ No

Are there specific hours the remote storage facility is accessible? ❐ Yes ❐ No

Is there a reading room for patrons in the building? ❐ Yes ❐ No

Are there security cameras or motion detectors in the remote storage facility? ❐ Yes ❐ No

How many doors give access to the remote storage facility? ___

How are the entrances secured? ___

Is there an alarm system or security on the entrances and exits? ❐ Yes ❐ No

How often does security patrol the remote storage facility? ___

When does the facilities and maintenance department clean the remote storage facility inside? ___

___

When does the buildings and grounds department clean outside the facility? ___

If the remote storage facility is below ground level, how often does someone check for unauthorized entrance or water damage? ___

Remote Storage Facility (Contractual Arrangement with Private Company)

Who can request materials from this remote storage facility? ______________________________

What is the turnaround time from request to receipt of materials from the remote storage facility? __________

How is access to the materials controlled? ______________________________

Does the remote storage facility perform background checks on its employees and its delivery personnel?
❒ Yes ❒ No

What type of security is present at the remote storage facility? ❒ Cameras ❒ Motion detectors ❒ Security guards

LOANS: INTRA-INSTITUTIONAL OR INTER-INSTITUTIONAL

Date of loan (also note in catalog record or file) ______

Duration of loan (from ship date to anticipated return date) ______

Exhibit dates ______

Date of return ______

Date returned to collection (also note in catalog record or file) ______

Item number, catalog number, or unique identifier ______

If the item has an RFID or microdot, how is the item identified? ______

Destination department or institution ______

Contact person ______

Phone ______

E-mail ______

Describe location of exhibit (type of exhibit case and environmental conditions)

______

______

Describe any special handling requirements ______

Describe any environmental requirements ______

Describe any special exhibition mounting requirements ______

Security

❐ Alarms

❐ Motion sensors

❐ Environmental sensors

❐ Other security devices ______

Is the item framed and hung on the wall? ❐ Yes ❐ No

How is the item secured to the wall? ______

Describe type and location of storage before and after the exhibit ______

______

Describe any defects or damage ______

How were the items returned?

❐ By courier

❐ By shipping company. Name of company ______

❐ Picked up by the lending institution. Name of staff member ______

Describe condition of returned item ______

EXHIBITIONS

Name of exhibition ______

Curator or contact person ______

Department ______

Phone ______

E-mail ______

Duration of exhibition

Anticipated arrival date for borrowed items ______

Anticipated return date for borrowed items ______

Location of exhibition ______

Hours open to the public ______

Environmental controls in cases and cabinets ❒ Yes ❒ No

Do they have alarms? ❒ Yes ❒ No

Security considerations for exhibition

❒ Alarms

❒ Motion detectors

❒ Broken glass detectors

❒ Particulate matter or smoke alarms

❒ Security cameras

❒ Security devices are hardwired into the electrical system

❒ Security devices are included on the emergency generator

❒ Security guards patrol during the day

❒ Security guards patrol at night

EXHIBIT ITEMS ON LOAN FROM OTHER DEPARTMENTS OR INSTITUTIONS

Date received (also note in exhibit database or file) __________

Date on which borrowed item was entered into exhibit database __________

Date returned (also note in exhibit database or file) __________

Date of confirmation from lending institution that item was received __________

Brief description of item __________

Property mark or unique identification number __________

If the item has an RFID or microdot, how is the item identified? __________

Lending department or institution __________

Contact person __________

Phone __________

E-mail __________

Describe condition of item __________

Describe special handling requirements __________

Describe environmental requirements __________

Describe special exhibition mounting requirements __________

Document any damage during transport __________

Date lending institution was notified of damage __________

Location of item on exhibit (case or cabinet number) __________

Location of item while awaiting exhibit (storage area) __________

Describe condition after exhibit __________

- ❐ Same as when received
- ❐ Damage as follows: __________

How were the items returned?

- ❐ By courier
- ❐ By shipping company. Name of company __________
- ❐ Picked up by the lending institution. Name of staff member __________

INSURANCE

Date insurance policy was reviewed and revised (minimum every two years) ____________________

Institutional Policy

Name of campus or administrative unit ____________________

Overall deductible ____________________

Deductible per loss ____________________

Types of losses covered ____________________

General Collections Policy

Name of department or building or campus ____________________

General collections ____________________

Total replacement cost ____________________

Per-volume replacement for

- Fiction ____________________
- Nonfiction ____________________
- Reference or noncirculating ____________________
- Audiovisual ____________________

ESTABLISHING DEDUCTIBLE AND CONTINGENCY FUNDS FOR INSURANCE AND LOSS

General Information

Maximum amount per loss institution can afford ______

Types of potential loss

- Theft by staff
- Theft by patrons
- Damage by patrons (mutilation of pages, tearing pages out, tearing texts from covers, attempting to remove security detection devices or RFID, defacing materials)

Number of campuses ______

Number of buildings the collections are housed in ______

Number of floors in each building the collections are housed in ______

Types of security

- Hours of security guards per day or per week ______
- Security gates or detection devices ❐ Yes ❐ No
- Alarms on doors and windows ❐ Yes ❐ No
- Alarms are activated ❐ always ❐ after hours ❐ during functions hosted by noninstitutional organization ❐ during functions hosted by institutional organization
- Company monitoring external alarm ❐ Yes ❐ No

Hours open per day ______

Hours open per week ______

Number of staff in building when open ______

Number of staff in building on weekends ______

Number of staff in charge ❐ during day ❐ in evenings ❐ on weekends

Number of staff or administration in nonpublic areas during weekdays ______

Potential and previous damage to building from outside

- ❐ Roof
- ❐ Walkways
- ❐ Stairways and stairwells
- ❐ External doors and other entrances
- ❐ Plantings

Potential and prior damage from internal hazards

- ❐ Water
- ❐ Fire
- ❐ Neglect
- ❐ Kitchens
- ❐ Mechanical rooms and closets
- ❐ Electric and gas meters and panels
- ❐ Stairways and stairwells

Who or What Is at Risk of Loss?

Types of collections

- ❒ General collections
- ❒ Special collections
- ❒ Rare books
- ❒ Archives—general and specific collections
- ❒ Institutional records
- ❒ Artwork
- ❒ Audiovisual
- ❒ Microformats
- ❒ Other formats
- ❒ Digital collections
- ❒ Proprietary or local databases

Date of last appraisal of art, rare books, or special collections ____________________

Do you have off-site storage of records of provenance and value for special collections, rare books, and artwork? ❒ Yes ❒ No

Insure at average cost and/or specific items ____________________

Locations where collections are stored

- ❒ In building
- ❒ In storage in building
- ❒ In storage on campus
- ❒ In remote storage (off campus or in another city)
- ❒ In other buildings with security
- ❒ In other buildings without security

Office records storage with destruction date ____________________

Office records storage with permanent retention ____________________

Value of building ____________________

Value of fixtures and furnishings ____________________

Office equipment

Type	Number	Value

Computers and other IT equipment

Type	Number	Value

Cars or other vehicles

Type	Number	Value

Risks

Institutional events

How often? ______

Average number of people? ______

Do members of the public attend? ______

Is there security for the building and the collections when these events occur? ❒ Yes ❒ No

Use of your building for noninstitutional events or activities

How often? ______

Average number of people? ______

Is there security for the building and the collections when these events occur? ❒ Yes ❒ No

Was insurance policy updated after the following?

New department created or new physical space allocated to collections ❒ Yes ❒ No

New storage area designated ❒ Yes ❒ No

New amounts or types of equipment purchased ❒ Yes ❒ No

New equipment installed in public areas ❒ Yes ❒ No

What types of deductions do you get for preventive actions (fire extinguishers, alarms, RFID, sprinklers, etc.)?

______

What preventive actions for theft, robbery, and damage to rare, special, and general collections and artwork reduce the cost of insurance? ______

INSURANCE: SPECIAL COLLECTIONS AND RARE BOOKS

Date collections were last appraised ______

Date the insurance rider was last reviewed ______

Name of collection or department ______

Type of format or material ______

Total replacement cost ______

Per-volume replacement cost ______

Items to be "scheduled" or itemized for insurance

  Minimum replacement value ______

  Total number of special collections or rare book items ______

  Location of "scheduled item" list ______

  Date the "scheduled item" list was last updated (minimum every three years) ______

Location of inventory ______

Location of accession or provenance files ______

Have these files been duplicated? ❐ Yes ❐ No

  Location of the original files ______

  Location of the duplicate files ❐ in-house ______

  ❐ outside ______

INSURANCE: ARCHIVES

Date collections were last appraised ____________________

For each archives collection

Name of collection	Location	Appraised value

Is there a record-retention schedule? ❒ Yes ❒ No

Where are materials stored for destruction? ____________________

Where are the materials for historical or long-term retention housed? ____________________

What is their overall value? ____________________

How are they insured? ____________________

Are any of the collections available in microform or as digital images? ❒ Yes ❒ No

Where are the use copies of these materials housed? ____________________

Where are the originals housed? ____________________

INSURANCE: ARTWORK

Date insurance policy was reviewed and revised (minimum every two years) ______

Total replacement cost ______

Per-item replacement ______

Items to be "scheduled" or itemized for insurance

- Minimum replacement value ______
- Total number of artworks ______
- Location of "scheduled item" list ______
- Date the "scheduled item" list was last updated (minimum every three years) ______

Locations where artwork is stored ______

Locations where artwork is displayed ______

Special coverage

- Insurance rider for travel to and from institution for exhibition? ❒ Yes ❒ No
- Insurance for artwork while on exhibition away from institution? ❒ Yes ❒ No
- Insurance for artwork from another institution while in storage or exhibit on your campus? ❒ Yes ❒ No
- Insurance rider for transportation of artwork for conservation or storage? ❒ Yes ❒ No

Transport of artwork

- By courier service
  - Is the courier bonded? ❒ Yes ❒ No
  - For how much? ______
- By institutional staff members
  - ❒ institutional vehicle
  - ❒ air
  - ❒ staff member's vehicle
  - Is the item insured while in transit by an institutional member? ❒ Yes ❒ No

Storage and conservation facilities

- Is the facility insured and bonded? ❒ Yes ❒ No
- If so, for how much? ______
- Is there security at the facility? ❒ Yes ❒ No
- Are there environmental controls at the facility? ❒ Yes ❒ No
- Are there safety devices (sprinklers, alarms, etc.) at the facility? ❒ Yes ❒ No

INSURANCE: COMPUTER HARDWARE

Name of department, building, or campus ________________

Overall deductible ________________

Deductible per loss ________________

Types of losses covered ________________

Minimum replacement cost ________________

Maintenance contract? ❒ Yes ❒ No

Types of equipment covered and their average replacement cost for like kind and function

- Laptops ________________
- Monitors ________________
- CPUs ________________
- Servers ________________
- Printers ________________
- Scanners ________________

INSURANCE: OFFICE EQUIPMENT

Name of department, building, or campus ________________

Overall deductible ________________

Deductible per loss ________________

Types of losses covered ________________

Minimum replacement cost ________________

Maintenance contract? ❒ Yes ❒ No

Types of equipment covered and their average replacement cost for like kind and function

- Copiers ________________
- Fax machines ________________
- Fax/copier/scanner/printer ________________
- Projectors ________________
- Audiovisual equipment ________________

Appendix B

Sample Forms

SPECIAL COLLECTIONS DEPARTMENT PATRON REGISTRATION FORM

Date ______________________________

Name ______________________________

Address ______________________________

____

Phone ______________________________

Identification
- ❒ Institutional faculty
- ❒ Institutional staff
- ❒ Student (graduate)
- ❒ Student (undergraduate)
- ❒ Public
- ❒ Institutional affiliation (if not local) ______________________________

Subject of Study ______________________________

Purpose
- ❒ Coursework
- ❒ Teaching
- ❒ Publication
- ❒ Dissertation/thesis
- ❒ Personal
- ❒ Other ______________________________

Subject of Study ______________________________

Purpose
- ❒ Coursework
- ❒ Teaching
- ❒ Publication
- ❒ Dissertation/thesis
- ❒ Personal
- ❒ Other ______________________________

USE AND RULES POLICY FOR SPECIAL COLLECTIONS, ARCHIVES, AND RARE BOOKS

(If you do not have your own policy you can use the guidelines below to design one.)

Patrons may use pencils only

Patrons may bring in pads of paper / loose sheets of paper / must use paper provided

Patrons may / may not bring in their own research materials for consultation in reading room

Patrons may / may not bring in folders of loose papers

Patrons may use electronic recording devices

- Laptop computer
- PDA
- Digital camera
- Regular camera
- Scanner
- Printer
- Cell phone
- Other devices

Itemize devices brought in

Confirm devices leaving with patron

All carrying cases, briefcases, and other containers must be stored along with coats in lockers.
Money / copy card / ID may be carried in container no larger than ______________________________

Staff / security will empty lockers at end of working day

Left items may be collected from security department within __________ days

USE POLICY OF SPECIAL COLLECTIONS DEPARTMENT

To safeguard the valuable and unique materials housed within the Special Collections Department, researchers are requested to observe the following rules:

1. No smoking is permitted in the Special Collections reading rooms. Food and beverages are also not permitted. Outer clothing, attaché cases, backpacks, and other similar items are to be left in the appropriate place.
2. Fountain pens, felt-tip pens, bottles of ink, or similar writing materials cannot be used. Researchers are asked to use pencils. Laptops and tape recorders may be used; please avoid disturbing other patrons.
3. Cameras or photographic equipment may be used with permission of the Department Head.
4. Patrons must fill out a registration card with their name, address, telephone number, and research topic prior to requesting materials. An out slip for each collection or item should be submitted to the person at the Reference Desk.
5. Materials must be handled with care; they must not be marked, torn, cut, folded, soiled, or traced over, nor should notes be written on top of materials, nor should materials be handled in any manner which might cause damage.
6. To assist the staff in maintaining the original order of the collections, researchers are requested to observe the following: use no more than ____ boxes at a time; use one folder from a box at a time; maintain the existing order of materials within each folder and box. If there is any doubt as to the order or if there is apparent damage, please notify the Reference Desk.
7. Materials may not be removed from the reading area. Materials may be photoduplicated in accordance with the policies and procedures of the Special Collections Department. The Department may set reasonable restrictions to protect fragile or damaged materials.
8. The use of certain manuscripts or other materials may be restricted by statute, by office of origin, or by the donors. The researcher must assume full responsibility for fulfilling the terms connected with any restricted materials. For the protection of its collections the Library also reserves the right to restrict the use of materials which are not arranged or in the process of being arranged, materials of exceptional value, and fragile materials.
9. Permission from the Library must be obtained in writing before manuscripts, diaries, correspondence, documents, and any other published materials from its collections can be published.
10. If permission to publish is granted, location of the material must be indicated in the work, and a complimentary copy presented to the Special Collections Department.

PUBLIC LIBRARY EXHIBITOR RELEASE FORM

In consideration for the opportunity to display works of art, artifacts, historical material, or other valuable items, hereinafter "Art," to the public, in designated display areas of the _______ Public Library, the undersigned owner of the Art described below agrees to hold the _______ Public Library, its Board of Trustees, Director, employees, and volunteers, harmless and to indemnify them from all claims of whatever nature arising out of the display of said Art at the Library, including loss, damage, or destruction of the Art, whether due to the negligence, active or passive, of the _______ Public Library, its Board of Trustees, Director, employees, and volunteers.

The Library will take reasonable steps to protect the Art and to display it in a manner which will attempt to ensure its safety, but the Library cannot and does not guarantee its safety or security.

All Art will be approved and placed for display by the Director subject to limitations of space, relationship to the theme of the show, and ability to mount or otherwise display the Art.

Art will be returned to the owner at the conclusion of the show, but not before. Art which is not picked up from the Library within one week from the conclusion of the show will become the property of the _______ Public Library.

A copy of this release will serve as a receipt for the Art by the Library and should be brought with the owner at the time the Art is picked up at the conclusion of the show for identification purposes.

Date on which show concludes and Art is to be picked up: ______________________________, 20______

Agreed to this ______________________________ day of ______________________________, 20______

Owner: ____
(print name)

____
(signature)

For ____________________ Public Library: ____
(print name)

____
(signature)

____
(title)

SPECIAL PERMISSION LOAN AGREEMENT

1. Special permission to take materials from the Special Collections (SPCL) Department may be granted in the following cases:
   a) Faculty members who want to show materials to students in the classroom
   b) University personnel for publication or exhibition
2. Other requests for special permission will be examined individually, and we reserve the right to deny special permission in all cases.

Other Institutions

All borrowers must be approved by the ____ Library; loans are made only to qualified museums or educational or research institutions whose missions are in the public interest and whose objectives are in concert with those of the SPCL Department.

General Policies

1. When on display, all objects borrowed must be credited to the SPCL Department, including any special wording as directed. Reproductions for publicity must also be credited.
2. All objects must remain in the condition in which they are received. They shall not be cleaned, repaired, retouched, treated, unfitted, remounted, reset, dissected, marked, copied (e.g., cast or replicated), or submitted to any examination or application that would tend to alter their condition except when specifically authorized by the Head, SPCL Department.
3. Damages, whether in transit or on the borrower's premises and regardless of who may be responsible therefore, shall be reported to SPCL immediately. No action is to be undertaken to correct the damage without the approval of the ____ Library.
4. The borrower may only photograph art object(s) for educational, exhibit catalog, record, or publicity purposes. Reproduction for sale is expressly forbidden except in the context of an exhibit catalog. The Head, SPCL Department, must approve all matters relating to commercial reproduction.
5. The borrower will undertake to provide protection from the hazards of fire, exposure to extreme or deteriorating light, extremes of temperature and relative humidity, insects, dirt, vandalism, theft, and mishandling or handling by unauthorized or inexperienced persons or by the public.
6. The borrower (except when exempted in writing) will insure the object(s) at the value stated by the SPCL Department, this insurance to be in force from the time the object(s) leaves the physical possession of the SPCL Department until it is returned. This shall be an all-risk policy subject only to the standard exclusions. The cost of insurance, special communications, security provisions, special packing, or any other incidental costs created in the loan will be paid by the borrower, unless waived by the appropriate program director.
7. When returning borrowed materials, they shall be packed in exactly the same manner as received and, in the case of art objects, with the same cases, packages, pads, wrappings, and other furnishings. Any changes must be specifically authorized in advance. Borrowers will be billed for the cost of packing materials if objects are returned in other than the original container.
8. Upon return, the objects are to be transported in the same manner as received and all costs for transportation connected with the loan will be paid by the borrower except in the case where other arrangements are

made. Any change in mode of transportation must be cleared by the Head, SPCL Department, and Risk Manager before release to the carrier.

9. Loans will be made for a specified time period as agreed upon and recorded on the loan document. To renew the loan, the borrower must request an extension in writing. Long-term loans shall be reviewed annually and, upon approval of the Head, SPCL Department, may be renewed for periods of up to another 12 months. All loans must be approved by the Head, SPCL Department, and the borrowing institution.
10. A signed copy of the Loan Agreement form must be in the possession of the SPCL Department before any physical transfer of object(s) is complete.
11. Objects or specimens are not be used as "hands-on" teaching aids unless specifically approved on the Loan Agreement form.

Specific Conditions

____

____

____

Items on loan ________________________________

____

Borrower's name ____________________ Date __________

Signature ________________________________

Institution ________________________________

Telephone number ____________________________

Head, SPCL name ____________________ Date __________

Signature ________________________________

Date borrowed ____ /____ /____ Returned ____ /____ /____ Initials __________

Special notes ________________________________

____

____

SPECIAL COLLECTIONS SHORT-TERM HOLD FORM

Call number ______________________________

OR

Record series number ______________________________

OR

Manuscript number ______________________________

Patron ______________________________

Address ______________________________

Telephone number ______________________________

Hold until ______________________________

- -

SPECIAL COLLECTIONS SHORT-TERM HOLD FORM

Call number ______________________________

OR

Record series number ______________________________

OR

Manuscript number ______________________________

Patron ______________________________

Address ______________________________

Telephone number ______________________________

Hold until ______________________________

SPECIAL COLLECTIONS DEPARTMENT OUT SLIP

Researcher name ______________________ Date __________

Collection name / title of book ______________________

Collection number / call number ______________________

Box number / volume ______________ Location ______________

Type of request
- ❐ Telephone
- ❐ Personal visit
- ❐ Correspondence

Type of record
- ❐ Photos
- ❐ Book
- ❐ University archives
- ❐ Manuscripts
- ❐ Other ______________________

Date Retrieved __________ Initials __________

Date Refiled __________ Initials __________

SPECIAL COLLECTIONS DEPARTMENT OUT SLIP

Researcher name ______________________ Date __________

Collection name / title of book ______________________

Collection number / call number ______________________

Box number / volume ______________ Location ______________

Type of request
- ❐ Telephone
- ❐ Personal visit
- ❐ Correspondence

Type of record
- ❐ Photos
- ❐ Book
- ❐ University archives
- ❐ Manuscripts
- ❐ Other __________

Date Retrieved __________ Initials __________

Date Refiled __________ Initials __________

TELEPHONE REQUEST FORM

Name of caller ______________________________

Phone number ______________________________

Additional information ______________________________

____

____

Staff member receiving request ______________________________

Date ______________________________

* * *

Request ______________________________

____

____

____

____

____

____

* * *

Referred to ______________________________ Date ______________

How handled ______________________________

____

____

____

____

____

CONSERVATION TRANSMITTAL FORM

Curatorial Custodian: Special Collections Department

Item description ❒ Book ❒ Manuscript ❒ Photograph ❒ Map ❒ Scrapbook
❒ Oversized drawing/sketch ❒ Other ______________________

Call no./MS no. ______________________

Author ______________________

Title ______________________

(Attach printout of bibliographic record if possible)

Problem ______________________

Shelf location ______________________

Collection/additional volumes ______________________

Treatment recommendations/needs ______________________

Exhibition intent ❒ Yes ❒ No Date needed ______________________

Insurance value $______________

(Needed for contract conservation work)

Signature of Special Collections staff transmitting item ______________________

Signature of Preservation staff member receiving item ______________________

Date ______________

Return to Special Collections

Signature of staff member returning item ______________________

Signature of Special Collections staff member receiving item ______________________

Date ______________________

Bibliographic record changed: Date ______________

Appendix

C

Resource Organizations

ORGANIZATIONS WITH INFORMATION FOR CULTURAL INSTITUTIONS ON THEFT AND SECURITY OR GUIDELINES FOR STORING COLLECTIONS

American Association of Museums
1575 Eye Street NW, Suite 400
Washington, DC 20005
Phone: 202-289-1818; fax: 202-289-6578
http://www.aam-us.org/index.cfm

American Library Association
(especially) Rare Books and Manuscripts Section of the Association
of College and Research Libraries, a division of the ALA
50 East Huron Street
Chicago, IL 60611
Phone: 800-545-2433; fax: 312-280-2520
www.ala.org

Association of Records Managers and Administrators (ARMA) International
13725 W. 109th Street, Suite 101
Lenexa, KS 66215
Phone: 913-341-3808 or 800-422-2762; fax: 913-341-3742
E-mail: hq@arma.org
www.arma.org

International Centre for the Study of the Preservation and
Restoration of Cultural Property (ICCROM)
Via di San Michele 13
I-00153 Rome, Italy
Phone: +39 (0) 6-585-531; fax: +39 (0) 6-585-53349
www.iccrom.org

International Council of Museums (ICOM)
Maison de l'Unesco
1, rue Miollis
75732 Paris cedex 15 France
Phone: +33 (0) 1-47-34-05-00;
fax: +33 (0) 1-43-06-78-62
E-mail: secretariat@icom.museum
http://icom.museum

Keys to Safer Schools.com
P.O. Box 296
Bryant, AR 72089-0296
Phone: 501-847-2596 or 877-978-7678 or
800-504-7355
http://KeysToSaferSchools.com

Library and Archives Canada
395 Wellington Street
Ottawa, Ontario ON K1A 0N4 Canada
Phone: 613-996-5115 or 866-578-7777;
fax: 613-995-6274
http://www.collectionscanada.ca/index-e.html

Ministry of Culture
900 Bay Street
5th Floor, Mowat
Toronto, Ontario M7A 1L2 Canada
Phone: 416-212-0644 or 866-454-0049
http://www.culture.gov.on.ca/english/index.html

Museums, Libraries and Archives Council (MLA)
Victoria House
Southampton Row
London WC1B 4EA United Kingdom
Phone: +44 (0) 20-7273-1444;
fax: +44 (0) 20-7273-1404
E-mail: info@mla.gov.uk
www.mla.gov.uk

National Archives
Kew, Richmond
Surrey TW9 4DU United Kingdom
Phone: +44 (0) 20-8876-3444
www.nationalarchives.gov.uk

National Archives and Records Administration
(NARA)
8601 Adelphi Road
College Park, MD 20740-6001
Phone: 866-272-6272; fax: 301-837-0483
www.archives.gov

National Park Service (NPS)
Museum Management Program
1849 C Street, NW
Room NC230
Washington, DC 20240
http://www.nps.gov/history/museum/

Society of American Archivists (SAA)
527 S. Wells St., 5th Floor
Chicago, IL 60607
Phone: 312-922-0140; fax: 312-347-1452
www.archivists.org

INSURANCE COMPANIES THAT COVER ARTWORK OR HAVE PROGRAMS FOR CULTURAL INSTITUTIONS

This list of organizations represents just a few of those available internationally. Inclusion on the list does not constitute a recommendation. For a select list of insurance companies for cultural institutions, see Jeanne Drewes's list of "Insurance Companies with Cultural Institution Policies" on the Library of Congress's Preservation Office website under "Emergency Preparedness, Insurance/Risk Management" (http://www.loc.gov/preserv/emergprep/insurancemain.html).

AIG Insurance
70 Pine Street, Floor 21
New York, NY 10270
Phone: USA: 877-638-4244; worldwide:
908-679-3150

Artinsure
6th Floor
55 Bishopsgate
London EC2N 3BD United Kingdom
Phone: +44 (0) 20-7578-7412;
fax: +44 (0) 20-7578-7102
www.artinsure.com

AXA Insurance Group
107 Cheapside
London EC2V 6DU United Kingdom
www.axa.co.uk

Cincinnati Financial Corporation
6200 S. Gilmore Road
Fairfield, OH 45014-5141
http://www.cinfin.com/home.asp

Inland Marine Underwriters Association (IMUA)
14 Wall Street, Floor 8
New York, NY 10005
Phone: 212-233-0550; fax: 212-227-5102
www.imua.org

Zurich in North America
105 E. 17th Street
New York, NY 10003
Phone: 917-534-4500
www.zurichna.com

ORGANIZATIONS THAT TRACK STOLEN ART OR THAT HAVE INFORMATION ABOUT ART AND SECURITY

Art Loss Register, Inc.
108 West 39th Street, Suite 506
New York, NY 10018
Phone: 212-297-0941 or 877-278-5677;
fax: 212-354-9020
E-mail: newyork@artloss.com
www.artloss.com

Art Loss Register Ltd. (UK Headquarters)
First Floor
63-66 Hatton Garden
London EC1N 8LE United Kingdom
Phone: +44 (0) 20-7841-5780;
fax: +44 (0) 20-7841-5781
E-mail: artloss@artloss.com
www.artloss.com

International Foundation for Art Research (IFAR)
500 Fifth Avenue, Suite 935
New York, NY 10110
Phone: 212-391-6234; fax: 212-391-8794
www.ifar.org

Lloyds of London
One Lime Street
London EC3M 7HA United Kingdom
Phone: +44 (0) 20-7327-1000
www.lloyds.com

Museum Security Network
POB 3213
3003 AE Rotterdam, The Netherlands
Phone: +31 (0) 10-2233897
www.museum-security.org

Stolen Art Recovery
c/o Saz Productions, Inc.
P.O. Box 5222
Chicago, IL 60680-5222
Phone: 708-456-4837
E-mail: saz@saztv.com
www.saztv.com

University of Wisconsin-Madison, "Actuarial Insurance and Risk Management"
http://www.bus.wisc.edu/asrmi/
(See links and resources for a list of insurance companies with listings on the Web.)

ORGANIZATIONS THAT PROVIDE SECURITY, RISK MANAGEMENT, AND INSURANCE FOR CULTURAL PROPERTY

Cultural Property Protection Group
www.cppgrp.com

Horizon Institute
www.horizon-usa.com

Steve Keller and Associates
www.stevekeller.com

Bibliography

American Library Association, Office for Intellectual Freedom. "CPPA, COPA, CIPA: Which Is Which?" 2006. http://www.ala.org/ala/oif/ifissues/issuesrelatedlinks/cppacopacipa.cfm.

American Library Association, Office for Intellectual Freedom. "RFID in Libraries: Privacy and Confidentiality Guidelines." 2006. http://www.ala.org/ala/oif/statementspols/otherpolicies/rfidguidelines.cfm.

Archives Association of British Columbia. *A Manual for Small Archives.* Vancouver: Archives Association of British Columbia, 1999. (See especially chapters 4 and 6.) Also available at http://aabc.bc.ca/aabc/msa/default.htm.

ARMA International and Society of American Archivists. *Sample Forms for Archival and Records Management Programs.* Mary Lea Ginn, consulting editor. Lenexa, KS, and Chicago: ARMA International and Society of American Archivists, 2002.

Association of College and Research Libraries. "Guidelines for the Security of Rare Books, Manuscripts, and Other Special Collections." 2005. http://www.ala.org/ala/acrl/acrlstandards/guidelinessecurity.cfm; and http://www.ala.org/ala/acrl/acrlstandards/securityrarebooks.cfm, as described in *College and Research Libraries News* 67, no. 1 (July/August 2006). (For other information and guidelines concerning rare books and manuscripts, see the ACRL website at http://www.ala.org/acrl/.)

———. "Guidelines Regarding Thefts in Libraries." 2005. http://www.ala.org/ala/acrl/acrlstandards/guidelinesregardingthefts.cfm.

Belcher, Michael. *Exhibitions in Museums.* Washington, DC: Smithsonian Institution, 1991.

Bingham, Karen Havill. *Building Security and Personal Safety.* SPEC Flyer 150 (January 1989). Washington, DC: Association of Research Libraries, Office of Management Services, 1989.

Blythe, Bruce T. *Blindsided: A Manager's Guide to Catastrophic Incidents in the Workplace.* New York: Penguin, 2002.

Bogdanos, Matthew, and William Patrick. *Thieves of Baghdad: One Marine's Passion for Ancient Civilizations and the Journey to Recover the World's Greatest Stolen Treasures.* New York: Bloomsbury, 2005.

Brady, Eileen E. *Library/Archive/Museum Security: A Bibliography.* 5th revised edition. Moscow, ID: Catula Pinguis, 1995.

Brand, Marvine, editor. *Security for Libraries, People, Buildings, Collections.* Chicago: American Library Association, 1984.

Breeding, Marshall. "Wireless Networks Connect Libraries to a Mobile Society." *Computers in Libraries* 24, no. 9 (October 2004): 29–31.

Bregman, Alvan. "Organizational Initiatives for Library Security: A North American Perspective." Paper presented at the conference "La coopération internationale au service de la sûreté des collections," May 14, 2004, sponsored by Bibliothèque nationale de France and LIBER. Available at http://www.bnf.fr/PAGES/infopro/journeespro/pdf/surete/bregman.pdf.

Breighner, Mary, William Payton, and Jeanne M. Drewes. *Risk and Insurance Management Manual for Libraries.* New York: Library Administration and Management Association, American Library Association, 2005.

Brown, Karen B. *Collections Security: Planning and Prevention for Libraries and Archives.* Technical Leaflet Emergency Management Section 3, leaflet 12. Andover, MA: Northeast Document Conservation Center, 1999, 2003. Also available at http://www.nedcc.org/resources/leaflets/3Emergency_Management/11CollectionsSecurity.php.

Burek Pierce, Jennifer. "The Scoop on Patron Privacy: Legislative Loopholes Have Made It Harder Than Ever for Librarians to Assure Users That Their Records Are Snoop-Proof." *American Libraries,* February 2005, 30–32.

Burke, Robert B., and Sam Adeloye. *A Manual of Basic Museum Security.* International Council of Museums, International Committee on Museum Security. Leicester, UK: DeVoyle, 1986.

Cannon, Alice. "Risk Management." In *Disaster Management for Libraries and Archives,* edited by Graham Matthews and John Feather, 41–72. Aldershot, UK, and Burlington, VT: Ashgate, 2003.

Chadwick, William E. "Special Collections Library Security: An Internal Audit Perspective." Simultaneously published in *Journal of Library Administration* 25, no. 1 (1998): 15–31; and *Management of Library and Archival Security: From the Outside Looking In,* edited by Robert K. O'Neill, 15–31. New York: Haworth, 1998.

Chaney, Michael, and Alan F. MacDougall, editors. *Security and Crime Prevention in Libraries.* Aldershot, UK, and Brookfield, VT: Ashgate, 1992.

Chaptman, Dennis. "Tag—You're IDed: UW Research Is Helping Share the Radio-Frequency Revolution." *On Wisconsin* 107, no. 1 (Spring 2006): 14.

Christoffersen, John. "Collector Pleads Guilty; Admits Stealing Rare Maps." Boston.com, June 22, 2006. http://www.boston.com/news/local/massachusetts/articles/2006/06/22/collector_pleads_guilty_admits_stealing_rare_maps/.

Copetas, Craig. "Brutal Trade of Rare Books." *The Age* (Australia), February 19, 2003. http://www.theage.com.au/articles/2003/02/18/1045330602055.html.

Courson, Paul, and Terry Frieden. "Sandy Berger Fined $50,000 for Taking Documents: Must Perform 100 Hours of Community Service." CNN.com, September 8, 2005. http://www.cnn.com/2005/POLITICS/09/08/berger.sentenced/index.html.

Courtois, Martin, and Claire B. Rubin. "Crisis, Disaster, and Emergency Management." *College and Research Libraries News* 63, no. 10 (November 2002): 723–27. Also available at http://www.ala.org/ala/acrl/acrlpubs/crlnews/backissues2002/novmonth/crisisdisaster.cfm.

Cowan, Alison Leigh. "A Rival Is Charged, and a Map Dealer Wants to Say, 'Told You So.'" *New York Times,* New York Region section, October 10, 2005.

———. "Theft Case Rattles Sedate World of Rare Maps." *New York Times,* Arts section, October 3, 2005.

Cox, Richard J. *Managing Records as Evidence and Information.* Westport, CT: Quorum Books, 2001.

Coyle, Karen. "Management of RFID in Libraries." *Journal of Academic Librarianship* 31, no. 5 (September 2005): 486–89.

Craig, Bruce. "Hundreds of Items Go Missing from National Archives." *Archival Outlook,* January/February 2005, 14. http://www.archivists.org/periodicals/ao_backissues/AO-Jan05.pdf. For more information about materials that are missing from the National Archives, see http://www.archives.gov/research/recover/.

Cravey, Pamela. *Protecting Library Staff, Users, Collections, and Facilities: A How-to-Do-It Manual for Librarians.* New York: Neal-Schuman, 2001.

Crews, Kenneth D. *Copyright Law for Librarians and Educators: Creative Strategies and Practical Solutions.* 2nd edition. Chicago: American Library Association, 2005.

Curry, Ann, Susanna Flodin, and Kelly Matheson. "Theft and Mutilation of Library Materials: Coping with Biblio-Bandits." *Library and Archival Security* 15, no. 2 (2000): 9–26.

Dennis, Brad. "Preventing Theft of Compact Discs at the Wyoming Branch Library: A Case Study." *Library and Archival Security* 16, no. 2 (2001): 41–47.

Dorge, Valerie, and Sharon L. Jones. *Building an Emergency Plan: A Guide for Museums and Other Cultural Institutions.* Los Angeles: Getty Conservation Institute, 1999. Also available at http://www.getty.edu/conservation/publications/pdf_publications/emergency_plan.pdf.

East, Dennis, and William G. Myers. "Get the Thief 'Out of the Business': Diary of a Theft." *Rare Books and Manuscripts Librarianship* 13, no. 1 (Fall 1998): 27–47. http://www.ala.org/ala/acrl/acrlpubs/rbm/backissuesrbmlvol13no1/eastmyers.pdf.

Fennelly, Lawrence J. *Museum, Archive, and Library Security.* Boston: Butterworths, 1983.

Foerstel, Herbert. *Surveillance in the Stacks: The FBI's Library Awareness Program.* New York: Greenwood, 1991.

Gandert, Slade Richard. *Protecting Your Collection: A Handbook, Survey, and Guide for the Security of Rare Books, Manuscripts, Archives, and Works of Art.* New York: Haworth, 1982.

Greene, Mark A., and Dennis Meissner. "More Product, Less Process: Revamping Traditional Archival Processing." *American Archivist* 68, no. 2 (Fall/Winter 2005): 208–63.

Gudsen, Neil. "Legal Liabilities in the Handling of Problem Patrons." *Library and Archival Security* 17, no. 1 (2001): 17–31.

Gutzman, Alexis D. *Unforeseen Circumstances: Strategies and Technologies for Protecting Your Business and Your People in a Less Secure World.* New York: AMACOM, 2002.

Harrison, Mary M., Alison Armstrong, and David Hollenbeck. "Crime in Academic Libraries." Chapter 7 in *Patron Behavior in Libraries: A Handbook of Positive Approaches to Negative Solutions,* edited by Beth McNeil and Denise J. Johnson. Chicago: American Library Association, 1996.

Howie, F., editor. *Safety in Museums and Galleries.* London: Butterworths, 1987. (Special supplement to the *International Journal of Museum Management and Curatorship.*)

Huntsberry, J. Steve. "Viva Blumberg: Lessons Learned." Museum Security. http://www.museum-security.org/blumberg-huntsberry.htm.

Inland Marine Underwriters Association, Arts and Records Committee. *Libraries and Archives: An Overview of Risk and Loss Prevention.* New York: Inland Marine Underwriters Association, 1993.

International Committee for Museum Security. *Museum Security and Protection: A Handbook for Cultural Heritage Institutions,* edited by David Liston. London and New York: Routledge, 1993.

Janus, Kristin M. "Securing our History." *Library and Archival Security* 17, no. 1 (2001): 3–15.

Jenkins, John H. *Rare Books and Manuscript Thefts: A Security System for Librarians, Booksellers, and Collectors.* New York: Antiquarian Booksellers' Association of America, 1982.

Kahn, Miriam B. *Disaster Response and Planning for Libraries.* 2nd edition. Chicago: American Library Association, 2002.

Kaplan, Diane. "Digital Cameras in the Reading Room." *Archival Outlook,* March/April 2006, 6–7, 25. http://www.archivists.org/periodicals/ao_backissues/AO-Mar06.pdf.

Kemp, Jane, and Laura Witschi, compilers. *Displays and Exhibits in College Libraries.* CLIP Note 25, sponsored by College Libraries Section, Association of College and Research Libraries. Chicago: American Library Association, 1997.

Keys to Safer Schools.com. "Fact Sheet: Dealing with Terrorism." http://www.keystosaferschools.com/Request_handouts_response_form.htm and http://www.keystosaferschools.com/Reports/Terrorism%20Fact%20Sheet-DC.pdf.

Kinsella, Eileen. "Why Wasn't 'The Scream' Insured? Museums Debate the Best Way to Protect Irreplaceable Works of Art." *ARTnews,* November 2004, 70.

Kopco, Mary. "Electronic Security Systems at a Small Museum: The Adams Memorial Museum Case Study." *Collections Caretaker* 1, no. 2 (2002). http://www.collectioncare.org/pubs/v1n2p4.html.

Kurtz, Michael J. *Managing Archival and Manuscript Repositories.* Chicago: Society of American Archivists, 2004.

Laiming, Susan, and Paul Laiming. *Insurances for the Public Library.* Chicago: Illinois Library Trustee Association, 1986.

Larson, Cindy. "Library on Guard with Old Books: Collectors Are Trying to Acquire Some Simple but Nostalgic Volumes." *Fort Wayne News Sentinel,* August 25, 2006, 1A.

Laye, John. *Avoiding Disaster: How to Keep Your Business When Catastrophe Strikes.* New York: John Wiley, 2002.

Layne, Stevan P. *The Cultural Property Protection Manual.* Denver: Layne Consultants International, 2005.

Lichtblau, Eric. "A Kerry Adviser Leaves the Race over Missing Documents." *New York Times,* Politics section, July 21, 2004.

Lincoln, Alan Jay, and Carol Zall. *Crime in the Library: A Study of Patterns, Impact, and Security.* New York: R. R. Bowker, 1984.

———. *Library Crime and Security: An International Perspective.* Lincoln, NY: Haworth, 1987.

Lueder, Dianne, and Sally Webb. *Administrator's Guide to Library Building Maintenance.* Chicago: American Library Association, 1992. See especially chapter 8, "Safety Considerations," and chapter 9, "Emergency Preparedness and Disaster Recovery."

MacDougall, Alan. "Security in Libraries." In *International Encyclopedia of Information and Library Science,* 572–74. 2nd edition. Edited by John Feather and Paul Sturges. London: Routledge, 2003.

Martin, Abigail Leab. "The Saying and the Doing: The Literature and Reality of Theft Prevention Measures in U.S. Archives—Part 1." *Library and Archival Security* 15, no. 2 (2000): 27–65.

———. "The Saying and the Doing, Part 2: The Real World and the Future." *Library and Archival Security* 16, no. 1 (2000): 7–35.

Martin, Susan K. *Insuring and Valuing Research Library Collections.* SPEC Kit 272 (December 2002). Washington, DC: Association of Research Libraries, Office of Leadership and Management Services, 2002.

Martineau, Kim. "Rare Documents Going Digital: Yale May Join Libraries Using Technology against Theft of Originals." *Hartford Courant,* January 15, 2006. Available at http://msn-list.te.verweg.com/2006-January/004165.html.

Maslin, Janet. "Traveling a Bumpy Road to Recover Stolen Art." *New York Times,* Books section, June 30, 2005.

Mason, Donald L. *The Fine Art of Art Security: Protecting Public and Private Collections against Theft, Fire and Vandalism.* New York: Van Nostrand Reinhold, 1979.

Mastio, Hilary. "Form Follows Function: The Development of the Internet as a Tool in Fighting Art Theft." Paper submitted for Course 366-10, "Law and Criminology," Law School, George Washington University, Washington, DC. 2000. Available at http://www.museum-security.org/arttheft-and-internet.html.

Matthews, Graham. "Crime in Libraries." In *International Encyclopedia of Information and Library Science,* 111–12. 2nd edition. Edited by John Feather and Paul Sturges. London: Routledge, 2003.

Matthews, Graham, and John Feather, editors. *Disaster Management for Libraries and Archives.* Aldershot, UK, and Burlington, VT: Ashgate, 2003.

McNeil, Beth, and Denise J. Johnson. *Patron Behavior in Libraries: A Handbook of Positive Approaches to Negative Solutions.* Chicago: American Library Association, 1996.

Mellgren, Doug. "Norwegian Police Find Stolen Munch Paintings." *Columbus Dispatch,* Arts section, September 1, 2006, B6.

Ministry of Culture (Ontario). "Museum Insurance." Note 5 in "Ontario Museum Notes." http://www.culture.gov.on.ca/english/heritage/museums/munote5.htm.

Minow, Mary. "Lawfully Surfing the Net: Disabling Public Library Internet Filters to Avoid More Lawsuits in the United States." *First Monday* 9, no. 4 (April 2004). http://firstmonday.org/issues/issue9_4/minow/index.html.

Mintzer, Fred, Jeffrey Lotspiech, and Norishige Morimoto. "Safeguarding Digital Library Contents and Users: Digital Watermarking." *D-Lib Magazine,* December 1997. http://www.dlib.org/dlib/december97/ibm/12lotspiech.html.

Mitroff, Ian I., and Murat C. Alpaslan. "Preparing for Evil." *Harvard Business Review,* April 2003, 109–15.

Morgan, Ian. "Librarian to Be Sentenced over Rare Book Thefts." 24dash.com, August 25, 2006. http://www.24dash.com/content/news/viewNews.php?navID=2&newsID=9668.

Museums, Libraries and Archives Council. *Insurance for Museums.* London: Museums, Libraries and Archives Council, 2004. First published by the Museums and Galleries Commission in 2000. Available at http://www.mla.gov.uk/resources/assets//R/risk_insurance_pdf_5879.pdf.

———. *Security in Museums, Archives and Libraries.* London: Resource and Museums, Libraries and Archives Council, 2002.

National Park Service, Museum Management Program. "Conserve O Grams." http://www.nps.gov/history/museum/publications/conserveogram/cons_toc.html.

———. *Museum Handbook.* Washington, DC: Government Printing Office, 2006. See part 1, "Museum Collections." http://www.nps.gov/history/museum/publications/handbook.html.

National Preservation Office, British Library. *Security Matters: Carrying Out a Library Security Survey and Drafting a Security Policy.* Leaflet series, August 1992. http://www.bl.uk/services/npo/pdf/security.pdf.

———. *Security Matters: Designing Out Crime.* Leaflet series, August 1996. http://www.bl.uk/services/npo/pdf/designing.pdf.

———. *Security Matters: How to Deal with Criminal and Anti-social Behaviour.* Leaflet series, April 1994. http://www.bl.uk/services/npo/pdf/criminal.pdf.

Nelson, Sandra, and June Garcia. *Creating Policies for Results: From Chaos to Clarity.* Chicago: American Library Association, 2003.

Ohio Attorney General. *Ohio's Concealed Carry Law.* (Ohio's H.B. 12). Columbus, OH. http://www.ag.state.oh.us/le/prevention/pubs/cc_booklet20040319-72.pdf.

O'Neill, Robert K., editor. *Management of Library and Archival Security: From the Outside Looking In.* New York: Haworth, 1998. (A collection of articles from the *Journal of Library Administration* 25, no. 1 [1998]).

Pitman, Bonnie. "Muses, Museums, and Memories." In "America's Museums," special issue, *Daedalus* 128, no. 3 (Summer 1999): 1–31.

Polk, Milbry, and Angela M. H. Schuster, editors. *The Looting of the Iraq Museum, Baghdad: The Lost Legacy of Ancient Mesopotamia.* New York: Harry N. Abrams, 2005.

Power, Peter G. "Manage a Crisis, Don't Recover from Disaster." *Contingency Planning and Management Online,* January 2003, 22–26.

Purcell, Aaron D. "Abstractions of Justice: The Library of Congress's Great Manuscripts Robbery, 1896–1897." *American Archivist* 62, no. 2 (Fall 1999): 325–45.

Putnam, Laurie. "By Choice or by Chance: How the Internet Is Used to Prepare for, Manage, and Share Information about Emergencies." *First Monday* 7, no. 11 (November 2002). http://firstmonday.org/issues/issue7_11/putnam/index.html.

"Radio Frequency ID Development and Debate Continue." *Library and Archival Security* 19, no. 1 (2004): 69–70.

RBMS Publications Committee, Rare Books and Manuscripts Section, Association of College and Research Libraries. *Your Old Books.* Chicago: American Library Association, 2005. Also available at http://www.rbms.info/yob.shtml.

Ritzenthaler, Mary Lynn. *Preserving Archives and Manuscripts.* Chicago: Society of American Archivists, 1994.

Roth, James M. "Reclaiming Pieces of Camelot: How NARA and the JFK Library Recovered Missing Kennedy Documents and Artifacts." *Prologue* 38, no. 2 (Summer 2006).

http://www.archives.gov/publications/prologue/2006/summer/camelot.html.

Rubin, Rhea Joyce. *Defusing the Angry Patron: A How-to-Do-It Manual for Librarians.* New York: Neal-Schuman, 2000.

Rudewicz, Frank E. "The Road to Rage." *Security Management,* February 2004, 41–44, 46, 49.

Russell, Carrie. *Complete Copyright: An Everyday Guide for Librarians.* Chicago: American Library Association, 2004.

Sabba, C. V. "International Art Crimes Investigators." 2006. http://www.yourbrushwiththelaw.com/heat.htm.

Sanders, Ken. "To Catch a Thief: On the Trail of a Rogue Collector." *OP Magazine* 1, no. 6 (November/December 2003): 10–16.

Sarkodie-Mensah, Kwasi, editor. *Helping the Difficult Library Patron: New Approaches to Examining and Resolving a Long-Standing and Ongoing Problem.* New York: Haworth, 2002.

Sherbine, Karen. "Closing the Book on Library Losses." *Best's Review: Property/Casualty* 92, no. 4 (August 1992): 64–68.

Shuman, Bruce A. *Case Studies in Library Security.* Westport, CT: Libraries Unlimited, 2002.

———. *Library Security and Safety Handbook: Prevention, Policies, and Procedures.* Chicago: American Library Association, 1999.

Smith, Elizabeth H., and Lydia Olszak. "Treatment of Mutilated Art Books: A Survey of Academic ARL Institutions." *Library Resources and Technical Services* 41, no. 11 (January 1997): 7–16.

Smith, Kitty. *Serving the Difficult Customer: A How-to-Do-It Manual for Library Staff.* New York: Neal-Schuman, 1993.

Soete, George J., and Glen Zimmerman. *Management of Library Security.* SPEC Kit 247 (July 1999). Washington, DC: Association of Research Libraries, Office of Leadership and Management Services, 1999.

Solving Difficult Situations (video recording). Towson, MD: Library Video Network, 2003.

Spiel, Robert E., Jr. *Art Theft and Forgery Investigation: The Complete Field Manual.* Springfield, IL: Charles C. Thomas, 2000.

Stark, Bruce P. "The Archivist as Detective; or, The Case of Ledyard v. William Morgan." *American Archivist* 67, no. 2 (Fall/Winter 2004): 269–92.

Starr, Joan. "Libraries and National Security: An Historical Review." *First Monday* 9, no. 12 (December 2004). http://firstmonday.org/issues/issue9_12/starr/.

State Library of Ohio. "Sample Library Policy Statements." http://winslo.state.oh.us/publib/policies.html.

Swartzburg, Susan Garretson, Holly Bussey, and Frank Garretson. "Safety, Security, Emergency Planning and Insurance." In *Libraries and Archives: Design and Renovation with a Preservation Perspective.* Metuchen, NJ: Scarecrow, 1991.

Switzer, Teri R. *Safe at Work? (sic): Library Security and Safety Issues.* Lanham, MD, and London: Scarecrow, 1999.

Tétreault, J. *Airborne Pollutants in Museums, Galleries, and Archives: Risk Assessment, Control Strategies, and Preservation Management.* Ottawa: Canadian Conservation Institute, 2003.

Teygeler, René. "Writing a Disaster Plan: Identifying Risk." In *Preparing for the Worst, Planning for the Best: Protecting our Cultural Heritage from Disaster,* edited by Joanna G. Wellheiser and Nancy E. Gwinn, 137–45. Munich: K. G. Saur, 2005.

Thenell, Jan. *The Library's Crisis Communications Planner: A PR Guide to Handling Every Emergency.* Chicago: American Library Association, 2004.

Thomson, Garry. *The Museum Environment.* 2nd edition. In association with the International Institute for Conservation of Historical and Artistic Works. London and Boston: Butterworths, 1986.

To Preserve and Protect: The Strategic Stewardship of Cultural Resources. Washington, DC: Government Printing Office, 2002. Essays from the symposium held at the Library of Congress, October 30–31, 2000. Also published as *The Strategic Stewardship of Cultural Resources: To Preserve and Protect,* edited by Angela T. Merrill (New York: Haworth, 2003); and copublished simultaneously as *Journal of Library Administration* 38, nos. 1/2 and 3/4, 2003.

Totka, Vincent A., Jr. "Preventing Patron Theft in the Archives: Legal Perspectives and Problems." *American Archivist* 56, no. 4 (Fall 1993): 664–72.

Trinkaus-Randall, Gregor. *Protecting Your Collections: A Manual of Archival Security.* Chicago: Society of American Archivists, 1995.

Turner, Anne M. *It Comes with the Territory: Handling Problem Situations in Libraries.* Revised edition. Jefferson, NC: McFarland, 2004.

United States Access Board. "ADA Accessibility Guidelines for Buildings and Facilities (ADAAG)." http://www.access-board.gov/adaag/html/adaag.htm#lib. Section 8 of the ADAAG is concerned specifically with libraries, as described and in compliance with 5 U.S.C. 552(a) and 1 C.F.R. part 51.

United States Environmental Protection Agency and United States Department of Health and Human Services. *Building Air Quality: A Guide for Building Owners and Facility Managers.* Washington, DC: Government Printing Office, 1991. Also available at http://www.cdc.gov/niosh/baqtoc.html.

United States National Institute of Occupational Safety and Health. *The Workplace: A Comprehensive Study.* Washington, DC: National Institute of Occupational Safety and Health, 1997.

Vamos, Robert. "Psst. Your Shiny New Passport Has a Computer Virus." C/Net, *Security Watch* (March 17, 2006). http://reviews.cnet.com/4520-3513_7-6466679-1.html.

Watkins, Michael D., and Max H. Bazerman. "Predictable Surprises: The Disasters You Should Have Seen Coming." *Harvard Business Review,* March 2003, 72–80.

Weessies, Kathleen. "The $ecret Inside Your Library's Atlases: Reexamine Your Collection and How to Protect It—before Someone Else Does." *American Libraries,* October 2003, 49–51.

Wellheiser, Joanna G., and Nancy E. Gwinn, editors. *Preparing for the Worst, Planning for the Best: Protecting our Cultural Heritage from Disaster.* Munich: K. G. Saur, 2005. Proceedings of a conference sponsored by the IFLA Preservation and Conservation Section, the IFLA Core Activity for Preservation and Conservation, and the Council on Library and Information Resources with the Akademie der Wissenschaften and the Staatsbibliothek zu Berlin, and held in Berlin, July 30–August 1, 2003.

Why Records Management? Gartner, NC: PRISM International, 2004.

Willis, Mark R. *Dealing with Difficult People in the Library.* Chicago: American Library Association, 1999.

Wood, Molly. "RFID: Bring It On." C/Net, *The Buzz Report* (February 2005). http://www.cnet.com/4520-6033_1-6223038-1.html.

Wythe, Deborah, editor. *Museum Archives: An Introduction.* 2nd edition. Chicago: Society of American Archivists, Museum Archives Section, 2004.

Yahn, Steve. "Modern Masters of Fine Art Risk." *Risk and Insurance,* November 1, 2004. Available at http://findarticles.com/p/articles/mi_m0BJK/is_14_15/ai_n7636641.

Yeide, Nancy H., Konstantin Akinsha, and Amy L. Walsh. *The AAM Guide to Provenance Research.* Washington, DC: American Association of Museums, 2001.

Index